INTERVI... ...ROM ...HE CANADIAN FILM WORLD

ESSAY SERIES 47

Canadä

ONTARIO ARTS COUNCIL
CONSEIL DES ARTS DE L'ONTARIO

Guernica Editions Inc. acknowledges support of
The Canada Council for the Arts.
Guernica Editions Inc. acknowledges support of the Ontario Arts Council.
Guernica Editions Inc. acknowledges the financial support of the
Government of Canada through the Book Publishing Industry Development
Program (BPIDP).

ANGELA BALDASSARRE

REEL CANADIANS

INTERVIEWS FROM THE CANADIAN FILM WORLD

GUERNICA

TORONTO·BUFFALO·CHICAGO·LANCASTER (U.K.)

2003

Antonio D'Alfonso, editor
Guernica Editions Inc.
P.O. Box 117, Station P, Toronto (ON), Canada M5S 2S6
2250 Military Road, Tonawanda, N.Y. 14150-6000 U.S.A.

Distributors:
University of Toronto Press Distribution,
5201 Dufferin Street, Toronto, (ON), Canada M3H 5T8

Gazelle Book Services, Falcon House, Queen Square,
Lancaster LA1 1RN U.K.

Independent Publishers Group,
814 N. Franklin Street, Chicago, Il. 60610 U.S.A.

First edition.
Typesetting by Selina.
Printed in Canada.

Legal Deposit – First Quarter
National Library of Canada
Library of Congress Catalog Card Number: 2002113557
National Library of Canada Cataloguing in Publication
Baldassarre, Angela
Reel Canadians : interviews from the Canadian film world / Angela
Baldassarre.
ISBN 1-55071-165-2
1. Motion picture producers and directors – Canada – Interviews. I. Title.
PN1993.5.C3B52 2002   791.43'0233'092271 C2002-904866-4

CONTENTS

TO ARIANNA

INTRODUCTION

In my first collection of interviews, *The Great Dictators: Interviews with Directors of Italian Descent,* I attempted to convey the wonderfully enlightened and expressive approach to studying the human heart that filmmakers of Italian origin have become so famous for. But with Canadians, be they actors, directors or producers, the challenge was very different.

The subjects of this collection have very little in common with each other, except for the fact that they have lived in Canada at one stage in their lives. To weave a connecting thread proved difficult but not impossible. Canada is famous for its comedians, and through my interviews with Mike Myers, Dan Aykroyd, Scott Thompson and Catherine O'Hara I hoped to shed some light on these popular professional lives. As for the superstars, David Cronenberg, James Cameron, Keanu Reeves, Sarah Polley and Atom Egoyan proved that fame and power couldn't cloud a Canuck heart. Then we have the independents – Bruce McDonald, Jerry Ciccoritti, Francois Girard, Jennifer Baichwal, Louis Belanger, Jeremy Podeswa, Vincenzo Natali and Clement Virgo – whose visions have enriched the Canadian cinematic landscape forever. These interviews were conducted over a ten-year period as I was working as a film journalist for several Canadian and international publications. And even though some of the films mentioned in the book are available to us today only on DVD or VHS formats, the spirit in which they were made is very much relevant in the words of its filmmakers and actors.

Canadian cinema has been a misunderstood beast in the jungle of international moviemaking for decades, prompting critics and essayists worldwide into writing endless essays about "our" style and sensibilities. This scribe purports to attempt no such gargantuan task. Instead, I let the artists speak for themselves in the hopes they could shed some light on what makes our culture so marvelously unique.

DAN AYKROYD

Blues Brothers 2000

Eighteen years after the events of the first Blues Brothers film, Elwood Blues is out of jail yet again, and finds himself put on another Mission from God to raise money for a good cause. But added into the confusion is the surfacing of Jake's long-lost Blues brother Cabel who's grown up to be a by-the-book police officer. With the help of a strip-joint bartender (John Goodman) Elwood must raise money for a children's hospital wing and to do so he reforms the band, for a Battle of the Bands in New Orleans, but not before running afoul of the cops, the Russian mob, and a rabid right-wing militia group.

Thus is the concept of *Blues Brothers 2000* which obviously doesn't only reprise the plot of the 1980 film, but also the director, John Landis, and many of the stars including Dan Aykroyd as Elwood and singers Aretha Franklin, James Brown, B.B. King, Clarence Clemons and others. Missing, unfortunately, is the second half of the rhythm and blues duo, John Belushi, who died from a drug overdose in 1982.

"After John died I thought that would be it," says Aykroyd on why he agreed to make a sequel to their movie. "But right after, I met this friend, Isaac Tigrett, who had lost two brothers to tragic circumstances, and his grief was so much bigger than mine could ever be. He helped me to get over John's death."

Aykroyd ended up becoming partners with Tigrett in the Hard Rock Cafe enterprise east of the Mississippi which they would eventually sell for a small fortune. "So I'm out of that, but every time we opened a Hard Rock Cafe, the Blues Brothers band came together. The original band," continues Aykroyd. "For a while our co-singer was Sam Moore of Sam and Dave. Then the band asked if we would license them the name so they could tour. Judy [John's wife] and I said, 'Go for it'; we get a small percentage of the take. I go out and play the harp sometimes. We do 'Soul Man' and 'Knock on Wood.' We rip the house apart."

Born in Ottawa, Ontario, forty-six years ago, Aykroyd grew up in a religious family. As the black sheep he got expelled from his Catholic seminary school but managed to continue his studies at Carleton University in Ottawa. While there he studied a variety of disciplines such as psychology, political science and criminal sociology, and became a member of the campus theatre/drama club, Sock 'n' Buskin. Aykroyd would drop out of college to pursue a career in comedy by joining Toronto's Second City comedy troupe. (He received an honourary Doctorate from Carleton University in 1994.)

"If it hadn't been for Carleton, The Blues Brothers movie would never have been made," laughs Aykroyd.

Although Second City allowed him to develop his comic skills, he would accept fellow Canadian Lorne Michaels' offer to take part of his new television sketch comedy show, *Saturday Night Live*. Along with Second City colleagues Bill Murray and Gilda Radner, Aykroyd moved to New York in 1975 and within months he became a household name. Teaming up with longtime buddy Belushi, he would create many of the show's most hilarious characters (Blues Brothers), as well as The Coneheads, Fred Jarvin: Male Prostitute, and those "wild and crazy guys" – the Czechoslovakian Playboys – with Steve Martin.

"I don't know why I make people laugh," says Aykroyd. "John Cleese once said that he used to think that comedy was watching something outrageous happen to somebody, but he then decided that what was really funny was watching someone watch something outrageous happen to someone."

Aykroyd would make three films with Belushi before the comedian's untimely death, following which most people believed Aykroyd would be unable to pursue movies on his own. He proved everyone wrong with terrific performances in *Trading Places, Spies Like Us* and *Ghostbusters* as well as excellent dramatic roles in *Driving Miss Daisy* and more recently, *Grosse Pointe Blank*.

Aside from a busy movie career, Aykroyd dabbles quite frequently in music as well. Following the release of the original Blues Brothers movie, he recorded two albums, *Briefcase Full of Blues* and *Made in America,* and has hosted a radio show for CBS as his Elwood Blues character.

"I'm a great emcee-front man and I can move onstage," he answers when asked to rate his musical abilities. "It's funny and exciting to see a man of 200-plus pounds moving in such a way that it looks like he knows reasonably well where he's going and he's not going to hurt people."

Once engaged to Carrie Fisher, Aykroyd is the father of two daughters by wife Donna Dixon, whom he met on the set of *Spies Like Us*. A police buff (perhaps because his grandfather was a Mountie) Aykroyd rides an Ontario Provincial Police motorcycle, collects police badges, and sometimes rides shotgun with detectives in squad cars.

"I think in a previous life I used to be a cop," he jokes. "But I don't have the right stuff. These guys are amazing. I couldn't do what they're doing."

Although he's considered a major American star, Aykroyd has always held a special place in the hearts and minds of Canadians. While he works in the United States primarily, he still makes time to return and develop work for the CBC, one of which is *Psi Factor*, a series exploring supernatural phenomena. Having been interested in the supernatural since childhood (his brother Peter is a psychic researcher) Aykroyd has amassed an extensive collection of books on the subject and is one of the show's major writers/researchers.

Regardless of which road Aykroyd decides to branch into during his career, he'll always be remembered, like his Blues Brothers co-creator John Belushi, as an integral part of comic history.

"That's the bad news," laughs Aykroyd. "With all the technology today, they'll be able to do without us altogether. They can just animate us, even after we're dead. Then our grandchildren can fight over the rights to dear old dead grandpa's image."

Published in Access Magazine, *February 1998.*

FILMOGRAPHY

Born on July 1, 1952, in Ottawa, Ontario.

- *The Devil and Daniel Webster* (2002)
- *Hitting the Wall* (2001)
- *Pearl Harbor* (2001)
- *The Curse of the Jade Scorpion* (2001)
- *Unconditional Love* (2001)
- *On the Nose* (2000)
- *The House of Mirth* (2000)
- *Loser* (2000)
- *Stardom* (2000)
- *Diamonds* (1999)
- *Susan's Plan* (1998)
- *Antz* (voice, 1998)
- *Blues Brothers 2000* (1998)
- *Grosse Pointe Blank* (1997)
- *My Fellow Americans* (1996)
- *Feeling Minnesota* (1996)
- *Celtic Pride* (1996)
- *Getting Away with Murder* (1996)
- *Sgt. Bilko* (1996)
- *Rainbow* (1995)
- *The Random Factor* (1995)
- *Canadian Bacon* (1995)
- *Casper* (1995)
- *Tommy Boy* (1995)
- *A Century of Cinema* (1994)
- *Exit to Eden* (1994)
- *My Girl 2* (1994)
- *North* (1994)
- *Coneheads* (1993)
- *Chaplin* (1992)
- *This Is My Life* (1992)
- *Sneakers* (1992)

- *My Girl* (1991)
- *Nothing But Trouble* (1991)
- *Masters of Menace* (1990)
- *Loose Cannons* (1990)
- *Driving Miss Daisy* (1989)
- *Ghostbusters II* (1989)
- *Caddyshack II* (1988)
- *The Couch Trip* (1988)
- *The Great Outdoors* (1988)
- *My Stepmother Is an Alien* (1988)
- *She's Having a Baby* (1988)
- *Dragnet* (1987)
- *Spies Like Us* (1985)
- *Into the Night* (1985)
- *Nothing Lasts Forever* (1984)
- *Ghostbusters* (1984)
- *Indiana Jones and the Temple of Doom* (1984)
- *Doctor Detroit* (1983)
- *Trading Places* (1983)
- *Twilight Zone: The Movie* (1983)
- *Neighbors* (1981)
- *The Blues Brothers* (1980)
- *Mr. Mike's Mondo Video* (1979)
- *1941* (1979)
- *Love at First Sight* (1977)

LOUIS BÉLANGER

Post Mortem

Remind me never to move to Eastern Europe. It seems that there is an unusual trend happening in countries like Bulgaria, Russia and Romania where seemingly dead people, women in particular are inexplicably brought back to life after being raped.

"I have no doubt about that happening," says director Louis Bélanger who included one such scene in his directorial debut *Post Mortem*. "I know that it happened at least once, and since making the film I received a lot of e-mails from people who also had that experience. In fact the girl was not dead, and sent at the wrong place by lousy paramedics. The people in morgues have no medical background, they wouldn't know. The corpse was in the freezing room. If somebody gives you warmth, maybe one could wake up."

Kind of a far-fetched concept, but considering that stranger things have happened in the world, this isn't that surprising. Like it wasn't surprising for Bélanger, a renowned script doctor in Quebec, that *Post Mortem* would receive the accolades it got. At this year's Genie Awards it got nominations as Best Picture, Best Actor (for Gabriel Arcand), Best Actress (for Sylvie Moreau), and Best Director and Original Screenplay for Bélanger. The thirty-six year old director not only walked off with the Screenplay statuette, but also took the Claude Jutra Award for first film.

"To be honest, we had done test screenings of *Post Mortem* for other filmmakers, and they said, 'you have a film here,' " says the youthful-looking Bélanger. "I won the best director prize at the Montreal Film Festival, and I was up against Ettore Scola and Kurosawa, and winning over them I felt I had a chance at the Genies as well. Although this is my first feature, I'm not new to this job. I've won many prizes at video festivals in the past."

Post Mortem is a dark tale about single mother Laura (Moreau) who at night is a prostitute that robs her tricks. One night, however, she finds herself on the other side of the violent stick. Ghislain (Arcand) is a recluse who works at the morgue at night, and finds companionship in his music. Fate has it that Ghislain falls in love with Laura's corpse, and while violating her body brings her back to life. Convinced that they are meant to be together, Ghislain pursues his beloved despite her disgusted rejections.

"Five years ago, a director friend, Denis Chouinard, and myself disciplined ourselves to read the newspaper each morning," explains Bélanger on how the concept of *Post Mortem* came about. "Each time we found something interesting we would put it into the computer for future projects. In *Le Monde Diplomatique*, a French newspaper from Paris, I found this short article about a guy in Romania working at the morgue in Bucharest, who had made love to a dead woman who came back to life. Those sort of articles are usually written in an ironic and cynical way, the writer tries to make the story funny. I found this particular one quite dramatic.

"Here is a case where the thin line between good and

evil is difficult to draw. We have a common set of morals that help us judge a lot of things that happen in society, but an act like this one is very difficult to explain. Necrophilia is considered bad, and as a society we judge this sort of activity as being a very bad thing. But here we have the case of this bad thing that brings someone back to life. It's difficult for me to say whether what happened was evil."

Although the article didn't specify how this woman died, Bélanger decided to add some elements of his own. What if she who dies works in a dangerous field, doing this sort of work so she can offer her daughter a better life? What kind of life does this woman have during the day, she who at night robs tricks? What happens if we make this woman a mother who is a practicing Catholic (played in the film by Helene Loiselle)?

"So once I started to think out the characters, the story began to take shape," says Bélanger. "But here I was with a story where I can present a character to the viewer, and at the thirty-minute mark she's dead. This is unusual in cinema. The only movie I've seen this done is in *Psycho*. I was fortunate enough to bring her back to life thanks to necrophilia and redemption. This story has already been told in cinema, but this event, necrophilia, gave me the opportunity to tell the story in a special way."

That "special way" is dividing the film into three sections. First we have "Linda," where we follow the protagonist's daily routine with her five-year-old daughter during the day, and unknown men at night. "Ghislain" is the depressing reality of this pathetically lonely solitary character. And "Odious Felicity" deals with the aftermath of the "event," when Ghislain is desperate to begin a relationship with Linda, whereas the woman wants to take advantage of this second chance life has given her.

"I didn't want to make a film about necrophilia," explains Bélanger. "I felt that I could play with the expectations of the viewers and bring them along in a way they didn't know what was going to happen. You see, the viewer always tries to go faster than the film. I had the opportunity to fool the spectators, because nobody knows how it's going to end up. I'm not a guy that does a lot of fancy stuff with the camera. The film has to rely on a strong script, in fact once I was on the set I knew I had the best version of the script because I had been working on it for more than two years. It's like a puzzle, if you change a thing, it has resonation on the rest of the script. I worked a lot on how to tell the story."

Despite the explanations, however, one can't help but snicker at the thought that in modern-day Montreal, a woman can be left for dead at a morgue and revived through sex.

"I've done a few versions [of the film] where more exact medical scenes were included, but that was slowing down the pace, and readers of the script said that I was wasting a lot of time with those details," explains Bélanger. "The film is about the two people, and not about the believability of the necrophilia scene. What happens in the morgue is less interesting to me than what they're doing in their daily lives. The way the woman deals with the little girl is fantastic, and the way she earns her money is interesting. The way the man expects to find love in his life, the way he's convinced that if he finds this love he'll have attained a level of being that is shared by everybody else in society. You have this man working the night shift, who lives in this little apartment. The moment he finds love he suddenly feels comfortable at being in public. He feels alive."

Now that he is Canada's latest boy wonder, what's next in store for Bélanger?

"I'm kind of lost," he smiles. "I'd like to do something about my father. He used to own a gas station and I learned a lot about life at the gas station. So I want to make a movie about that. I also have all this footage I took when the Berlin Wall came down. I want to set the movie in the 1980s, so I can put the footage in. I want to make a parallel between the Berlin Wall, society changing, full-service gas stations turning into self-serve. But first I will do a documentary on the late Jean-Claude Lauzon [*Leolo*]. It'll be the first time I work on something where I don't write the script."

Published in Tandem Magazine, *April 2000.*

FILMOGRAPHY

Born in 1964, in Quebec.

- *Post Mortem* (1999)

James Cameron

Titanic

Los Angeles. James Cameron is ecstatic, but exhausted. He just flew back from Halifax, Nova Scotia, where he completed the last of his twelve deep-sea dives 12,000 feet under the surface of the Atlantic Ocean shooting the wreckage of the Titanic, and he's emotionally spent.

"Being down there in a submersible is incredible," says the forty-three year old director with a smile. "But we never lost track of the fact that it's a shrine. The area in which we were diving was the bow section of the ship and there was nobody on that part of the ship when it sank. The ship essentially broke in half and most of the people who died on the ship died on the stern section, which was about a mile away from where we were. When we finished our work we took nothing, we only photographed, and when we finished our last dive I came up after seventeen hours. We filmed all night and part of the day and in the afternoon, we went out on the fan tail of the ship with a wreath which was dedicated to the passengers and crew of the Titanic and dropped it overboard. There's something that happens to you when we are there. You get overwhelmed with this great sense of tragedy."

Indeed, Cameron was prepared to go through such emotional turmoil when he insisted that he acquire never-before-seen footage of the doomed ocean liner for his multi-million dollar movie, *Titanic*. And though he insists he took nothing from the wreckage, which, since its discovery in 1985, is not protected, he does admit to a minor accident.

"If the site is protected at all it's from salvage, citizens bringing those objects back from the U.S.," explains Cameron. "There have been two French expeditions, and one of them just pillaged the place and went through the debris field and picked up the china and wine bottles and brought it all over to France. In the movie I have characters looking for something on the ship, so we built a remotely operated vehicle that had arms on the front that looked like it was designed to physically take things. I got carried away on one of the dives and actually sent it inside the ship and we looked around at things no one had ever seen since the sinking, but in the process we got a piece of wood jammed in one of the thrusters and the ROV came back with a piece of the Titanic stuck in its motor which I now have."

Based on an original script by Cameron, *Titanic* begins in modern-day and flashes back to the fateful four days in 1912 leading up to the ship's sinking. Cameron adopted a handful of fictional characters that he mixed in with historical figures to tell what he calls an "epic love story à la *Romeo and Juliet*."

Rose DeWitt (Kate Winslet) is a seventeen year old upper-class American suffocating within the confines and expectations of Edwardian society. She is on the Titanic with her prissy fiancé (Billy Zane). After meeting free-spirited steerage passenger Jack (Leonardo DiCaprio) Rose discovers a wonderful world outside her gilded cage but her happiness with Jack is short-lived.

Obviously more than just a love story, *Titanic* will expose the many theories surrounding the ship's final hours such as the gaps of communication, absence of emergency procedures, and the ingrained privilege of the upper classes who were given priority on the insufficient number of lifeboats.

"The tragedy of the Titanic has assumed an almost mythic quality in our collective imagination," says Cameron. "But the passage of time has robbed it of its human face and its vitality. I hope that Rose and Jack's relationship will be a kind of emotional lightning rod allowing viewers to invest with their heart and imagination and make history come alive again."

Cameron also admits that what appealed to him about the Titanic was its technology and man's disillusionment with it.

"Not only disillusionment, but our tendency even beyond disillusionment to have faith in technology," says Cameron. "I can draw a pretty good parallel between the faith that they put in a ship like the Titanic in 1912, an almost unshakable faith that science and technology would lead us to a better age and a better life, with no penalty paid, and the current hype and hysteria about the information super-highway and how computing is going to bring us a brave new world. Which it probably will, by the way, but it's not without risks. I think people have to be very heads up about the risks."

Born, in Kapuskasing, Ontario, Cameron grew up in Niagara Falls before moving to California to study physics ("I wanted to be a marine biologist but then I found out how much money they made," laughs Cameron). He left his job as a machinist and truck driver and raised money from a consortium of dentists to produce a short film which would lead him to work with Roger Corman in 1980's *Battle Beyond the Stars*. After this he became second unit director on *Galaxy of Terror*, another Roger Corman film, and in 1982 he wrote the script for *The Terminator*, and a first draft of *Aliens*. Both films, which he would direct, would go on to gross hundreds of millions of dollars at box offices around the world. He would eventually direct other box-office breaking hits *The Abyss, Terminator 2* and *True Lies.*

Cameron, however, is realistic about the financial expectations of *Titanic* which lacks any big-name action talent like Arnie or Sly. But he's unfazed.

"My favourite movie of all time is *Doctor Zhivago*," says Cameron who has been married to director Kathryn Bigelow and producer Gale Anne Hurd, and who fathered a child by Linda Hamilton. "I wanted to make a movie that was just as epic and memorable, that's why I didn't want a *Towering Inferno* kind of cast. There have been no real good Titanic movies except for [Roy Baker's 1958's] *Night to Remember*. But even that was inaccurate in many ways. A lot was found out about the Titanic subsequently, especially since the wreck was discovered. Also *Night to Remember* was what we would call a 'docudrama,' all the characters in it were real people on the Titanic. It was sort of a retelling of history, slightly dramatized but pretty straight forward."

Although tired, Cameron is excited to head back to Halifax to start shooting the narrative part of the movie. But before he leaves he insists on telling me about an event that happened aboard the Keldysh, the Russian research vessel that took him on the dives.

"Most of the Russian crew had been there before. They had dived there previously," says Cameron as I accompany him to the elevator. "I had a tape of *Night to Remember* with me, and they had never seen it. So I had 100 Russian crew members packed into this little room watching the movie in English, and though they didn't even understand two thirds of it, half of them came out crying. A quarter of them couldn't work the next morning because they were overwhelmed about being there. That's how I feel right now."

Published in Access Magazine, *July 1997.*

FILMOGRAPHY

Born August 16, 1954, in Kapuskasing, Ontario

- *Ghosts of the Abyss* (2002)
- *Titanic* (1997)
- *T2 3-D: Battle Across Time* (1996)
- *True Lies* (1994)
- *Terminator 2: Judgment Day* (1991)
- *The Abyss* (1989)
- *Aliens* (1986)
- *The Terminator* (1984)
- *Piranha II: The Spawning* (1981)
- *Xenogenesis* (1978)

JERRY CICCORITTI

Boy Meets Girl

For nearly a decade Toronto director Jerry Ciccoritti (*Paris, France*) had been wanting to make a movie based on his Italian-Canadian experiences. Although he had several projects in mind, he knew it would be impossible to get anything off the ground for at least another year or two. Then the script for *Boy Meets Girl* fell on his lap.

"They sent me this script in November right after Thanksgiving, and I was just charmed by it," remembers Ciccoritti from the set of his film. "I liked it a lot; it appealed to something in me that I didn't know was in me. The cornball romantic film kinda evokes this old Hollywood romantic comedy feelings in me and I thought, God, this just might be fun to do. I had nothing planned for the winter, so I thought I'd jump in and do it."

The movie, which made its premiere at last year's Toronto International Film Festival, is finally getting its Toronto theatrical release this week, much to the relief of its young and charismatic director.

Set in Toronto's Little Italy (the College St. one), the story focuses on lonely and lovesick Angelina (Emily Hampshire), an Italian waitress who is unhappy because she's betrothed to a man she doesn't love. Meanwhile cynical writer Mike (Sean Astin) is ready to pack his bags and tour the world. Angelina doesn't speak English and Mike doesn't speak Italian, yet both their destinies are thwarted when Il Magnifico accidentally draws them together with his poetry. A very simple plot.

"That's it. It's really gossamer thin," agrees Ciccoritti. "It takes place over the last three days leading to Valentine's Day and in traditional romantic comedy set-ups a boy and a girl meet through convoluted circumstances. She thinks he's a romantic Italian poet which he isn't. He, in fact, hates romance and he thinks that she's single and available which of course she isn't. She has been promised to marry a guy from the old country since she was ten. So there's a lie that comes between them."

Boy Meets Girl contains some charming 1950s-style sets, and the familiar Italian love tunes featured throughout are deliciously melancholic. But it's important not to forget those seductive trysts between two of the industry's most respected actors, Joe Mantegna (who plays Il Magnifico) and Kate Nelligan (who plays his sexy lover Mrs. Jones).

"They are kind of the god and goddess of love," says Ciccoritti. "They come to Little Italy to spread a magical enchantment over the neighbourhood. Everyone falls in love. Love grows. Love is everywhere except with these two people who are caught up in a push-pull of should they be in love with each other or shouldn't they? Should they tell each other the truth or shouldn't they?"

If it all sounds very sweet, that's because it is.

"That actually informed a lot of my decision to do it," says Ciccoritti whose family hails from the Lazio region. "When I first got the script [by Timothy Lee and Doug Bagot] and I read it, I was charmed by it, but I thought it's very thin. Not shallow, but thin. I thought I'd like to do this and maybe make notes for a re-write and we can deepen the character conflicts and add some subplots, and I kicked it around for awhile. Then I thought, actually, that's the wrong way to approach this. Rather than just digging deep below the surface this thing needs to be decorated, it needs to be dealt up from the surface. Let's accept the simplicity and decorate it like a big beautiful cake."

Ciccoritti enjoys playing up the Italian aspect of the story by focusing on the ethnic locales, music and dialogue (although Hampshire's Italian is pretty bad), with some funny farcical moments. One of the movie's most enjoyable scenarios, in fact, occurs in a restaurant scene when two waiters (played by Alvaro D'Antonio and Frank Crudele) cause hilarious havoc.

But while the movie is pure fiction, Ciccoritti admits that he found symmetry with one of its characters.

"I identify primarily with the character of Angelina, the female lead, because she's caught between the two worlds," he says. "She's from Italy, barely speaks English and she feels ties to a foreign country, to a way of being brought up, to the past and yet her heart longs to set roots down in this new country and while she's caught between the men, the man from the old country and the man from the new country, she makes incorrect decisions. All her troubles come from this lack of self-knowledge, of not knowing who she is and where she belongs to. That was always there in that character, and I most identify, as most Italian-Canadians do, with that."

Published in Tandem Magazine, *January 1998.*

The Life Before This

Jerry Ciccoritti has managed to become a household name within the Toronto film community, but critical praise still seems to be eluding him despite some commercially pleasing fare (*Boy Meets Girl* delighted audiences at the Toronto International Film Festival last year). With his newest film, *The Life Before This*, Ciccoritti is venturing into more complicated territory betraying indications that he is developing into a more mature and interesting filmmaker. *The Life Before This* looks back on the lives of six individuals just hours before they walk into a coffee shop that is about to robbed.

Rumours have it that you and producer Ilana Frank drew inspiration for The Life Before This *from the Just Desserts tragedy.*

Wrong. Ilana and I came up with the idea together. About three years ago she and I were having lunch, just kicking around ideas for an interesting movie. And one of the ideas was to do something around questions of chance and fate that was revolving around the horrible tragedy at Just Desserts. It's not that we wanted to do the Just Desserts movie, but we were wondering about that poor woman when she woke up that morning making a very casual decision that day to go for coffee and a piece of cake and not realizing that she was going be killed. No one in that place knew that evening that that was going to happen. So we thought it was interesting to spin that off into different characters.

Why this kind of structure, present-past-present?

It's funny, I can't talk too much about it without giving away the movie. When Semi [Chellas, writer] had written the script with Ilana, by that point they had worked out the basic storyline. The two of them spent weeks deciding on these characters; there were dozens of characters before they settled on this particular group. And then when I read it I thought there was one thing missing; there's this one really important change that I think was really needed to keep it from being just a little clever construct. And I told them what that change should be and then everything else came together.

You also have an amazing cast: Catherine O'Hara, Stephen Rea, Joe Pantoliano. How did you manage?

Every good actor just wants a really good part. Truffaut once said that every actor should ask himself three questions before he accepts a role: are they going to get paid a lot of money, is it a good part, is it going to help their career? And if you don't get answers to all three it should be at least two out of three, and it should be the last two. And we had the second two in this case. It was a terrific script and everybody had a chance to stretch. Joe Pantoliano, for example, is always being cast as some kooky villain, and as brilliant as Catherine O'Hara is she usually gets offered the high comedy roles. All these actors read it and really jumped on board. The producer and I thought we shouldn't have standard auditions for it and just came up with names of people we thought would be perfect for it.

Compared to this, making Boy Meets Girl *seemed like a piece of cake. What challenges did* The Life Before This *pose for you?*

The challenges were, essentially, holding myself back. I firmly believe that the look and feel of the film has to be completely appropriate to what the story is. I'm not a big believer of "appliquéing" a directing style to it. I feel that to put a nice icing on a real bad cake may look nice to the eye but when you bite it, it sucks. *Boy Meets Girl* was about lushness and over-the-top romance and references to Hollywood movies and it had a completely fake and stylized look. This is a film about those very tiny, ephemeral acts and decisions that we make that are so small they almost go unnoticed but they have great repercussions in our lives. And I knew that any kind of over-the-top directing style would bury that, or conversely would underline it too much and make it pretentious.

Simplicity, then.

Yes, I felt this had to be an absolutely and vigorously simple movie where the colour scheme was simple, the camera moves, the editing. And even the acting was very, very simple. I thought that if I keep everything simple, and small, we'd have a natural tendency to want to read into something. Make it too big, and the audience sits back in their chair. It's almost the quieter you speak the more people lean in to listen to you. That's what I wanted to make. It was actually really hard to do, plus you have to watch your own natural tendencies to go wild with the camera.

It's nice that you've managed to sneak some Italian flavour into one of the segments of the movie.

It's funny. In the original version of that storyline it was a Wasp family, a small family. For almost a year it stayed the same. One night Ilana phoned me and said she wants to make it all Italian with a big family. But I told her that no one's going to believe that it was not my idea.

What's next?

Too many irons in the fire. The closest to me is a book called 1978, written by Daniel Jones who killed himself a couple of years ago. It's about the lives of a group of punk rockers in the 1970s Toronto scene. The dying days of that scene.

There were rumours that you were working on a movie about the internment of Italian-Canadians during World War II with Nino Ricci.

It's not true. I'm not doing a film on the internment of Italians with Nino Ricci. We kicked around the idea for awhile, but for various reasons we abandoned it although I'd like to work on it eventually. There is a great story on the Petawawa camp, but I'm not sure what it is. It is such a big story, you have to focus somewhere. It's not right to take it as a hook. It's early days for that still; I'm collecting data, and I'm hoping to start the script by next year.

Published in Tandem Magazine, *December 1999.*

FILMOGRAPHY

Born in Toronto, Ontario.

- *Chasing Cain* (2000)
- *The Life Before This* (1999)
- *Boy Meets Girl* (1998)
- *Paris, France* (1993)
- *Love & Die* (1988)
- *The Understudy: Graveyard Shift II* (1988)
- *Graveyard Shift* (1987)
- *Psycho Girls* (1985)

DAVID CRONENBERG

eXistenZ

That David Cronenberg is fascinated with the morbid and the macabre there's little question. The fact that this obsession is coupled with a preoccupation with science fiction is what makes his movies so unique and, especially, stylistically innovative. And although the topics of his movies are thematically varied, they are however all connected with a delicious anxiety about sexuality and modern life, transcending his work well beyond any specific genre.

With his new picture *eXistenZ* (the emphasis on the capital letters), Cronenberg has returned to his early sci-fi style featuring his first completely original screenplay since 1982's *Videodrome*. What makes this project particularly interesting is that the spark for the movie about a computer games creator who invents a controversial game which makes her the target of an assassination attempt occurred during a meeting with Salman Rushdie.

"It's the truth," says Cronenberg, fifty-six, from his office in Toronto. "But I probably had it in my head to want to do something that connected in one level or another with Rushdie's situation before I actually talked to him."

Cronenberg, in fact, met Rushdie in the summer of 1993 for a magazine article the filmmaker was writing on the author. It was during this conversation that the two discussed the consequences of reality clashes.

"I was fascinated by what was happening with him," remembers Cronenberg. "Him coming from the western tradition of literature and freedom of expression, and running into the wall of this Islamic religious militant understanding of what was prohibited and what was allowed. When I originally started to write the script I thought that we would never actually play this game that we were involved in. One of the things that I discussed with Rushdie was whether or not a game could actually be art. Could one create a game and actually be an artist? I started to think about my lead character being a game designer and she's on the run because of what she's created. I thought that I would never actually see the game that she was playing and it would be more about her being on the run, but as I started to write it I became more and more intrigued at what the game might be and how it connected with the themes of the film in general. So the whole focus of the film shifted somewhat."

eXistenZ is the name of the latest games system created by Allegra Geller (Jennifer Jason Leigh) which taps so deeply into its users fears and desires it blurs the boundaries between reality and escapism. After fanatics threaten to kill her, Allegra is forced to flee with the help of a loyal security guard, Pikul (Jude Law). But the lure of the game draws the fugitives into a dangerous predicament.

Although there are traces of virtual reality and computer science thrust within the concept, Cronenberg insists that his movie is not a VR flick, but a sci-fi one.

"I really think that all reality is virtual actually," explains the director. "The themes in my films in general are about being, the extent of which we create our own reality, so I don't think there are any absolutes in terms of reality. The most real thing is the human body, which is the primary fact of human existence. That's really more what the film is discussing than anything to do with computer games. For a filmmaker virtual reality is nothing new. Every time you make a film you are creating another reality."

In fact, Cronenberg insisted that his lead actors read up on existential philosophy while preparing their roles. The reason, he explains, is that the essential philosophy of the movie is a very existentialist one and that it was important the actors understood the philosophical underpinnings of the story in order to interpret it.

"At one point the Pikul character talks about the kind of game that you were born into and not knowing the rules and not understanding what the forces are that are around you even though some of them seem to want to kill you," says Cronenberg. "Allegra says, 'That sounds like my game,' and he says, 'That game is going to be hard to market.' She says, 'But it's a game that everybody's playing.' Of course I'm meaning life at that point, and the game that's in the movie is the game of life, it's the game of existence."

Born and raised in Toronto, Cronenberg was the son of newspaper columnist and professional pianist. After studying literature at the University of Toronto, he wrote some prize-winning sci-fi stories but soon turned his attention to filmmaking. His first commercial features (*Shivers, Rabid, The Brood, Scanners, Videodrome, The Dead Zone*) established him as a filmmaker who could create suspense through character and atmosphere rather than gore, although there's plenty of that in his films.

His remake of *The Fly* would be Cronenberg's first commercial hit, and critical acclaim would come with the psychosexual drama of twin gynecologists locked in a bizarre symbiosis, *Dead Ringers*. Controversy, and more acclaim, followed with his adaptation of William Burroughs' hallucinatory novel *Naked Lunch* and J.G. Ballard's sexually obsessive *Crash*.

And while no stranger to controversy, Cronenberg feels quite confident that *eXistenZ* will cause little stir.

"I think that's partly because it's safely imbedded in its genre," says the father of two teenagers. "The only reason *The Fly* was accepted was because it was a sci-fi horror movie and because it was a genre piece, even though it had a depressing ending and it's pretty tough to watch. If that hadn't been a genre piece it would've been a very tough sell. So I think *eXistenZ*, being a sci-fi movie won't be controversial. Whether it will be more popular than my last films, I've got very philosophical in an existentialist kind of way, I guess. It's in the lap of the gods."

Published in Access Magazine, *March 1999.*

FILMOGRAPHY

Born March 15 1943, in Toronto, Ontario.

- *Spider* (2002)
- *Camera* (2000)
- *eXistenZ* (1999)
- *Crash* (1996)
- *M. Butterfly* (1993)
- *Naked Lunch* (1991)
- *Dead Ringers* (1988)
- *The Fly* (1986)
- *The Dead Zone* (1983)
- *Videodrome* (1983)
- *Scanners* (1981)
- *The Brood* (1979)
- *Fast Company* (1979)
- *Rabid* (1977)
- *Shivers* (1975)
- *Crimes of the Future* (1970)
- *Stereo* (1969)
- *From the Drain* (1967)
- *Transfer* (1966)

HOLLY DALE

Blood & Donuts

Director Holly Dale has the most enigmatic expression on her face as she watches David Cronenberg deliver his bad-guy lines on the set of *Blood & Donuts*. Whether it's appreciation for the horror-movie director's acting abilities or bemusement for the scene's outcome, Cronenberg's character is killed by a vampire, it's anybody's guess. For some of us gathered in the basement of an old Pape Avenue church, however, watching the man responsible for terrifying us with his films finally getting his comeuppance, the scene is sweet vindication.

"He's very good in it," smiles Dale months later, shooting finally over. "I think that part of David really enjoys being the actor because he can be on the set and not have to worry about those things that directors have to worry about. It was quite exciting because, being a director, he understands acting."

Dale is more than just excited. She's elated that her first feature film is finally completed and she can't wait to have the public see it. After all, this is no ordinary Holly Dale picture. *Blood & Donuts* is her first major solo project without partner/collaborator Janis Cole, and her first non-documentary effort. A vampire movie, no less.

"I've always been attracted to different genres," explains Dale. "I do really believe that if you're going to raise stories to people and make people get the message, it's a wonderful thing to do it in a fantasy kind of way. What I was attracted to about *Blood & Donuts* was that it was a fantasy tale. The way I read the script, it was set in no particular time, in no particular place, it could Parkdale, it could be Regent Park, it didn't have a definition of this place in this city. It was a world all onto itself."

Written by Andrew Rai Berzins, *Blood & Donuts* is one of three films being produced by the newly-founded Feature Film Project, an initiative of the Canadian Film Centre. Starring Gordon Currie (*Alive, Dieppe*) as displaced vampire Boya, the film is a strange but humourous tale about love, friendship and survival. The movie also features Justin Louis (*Urban Angel*) as a cabbie, Helene Clarkson (*The Bambi Bembenek Story*) as a love-torn waitress, and Fiona Reid as the vengeful lover.

"Underneath, this is a very tender story about trading in loneliness for friendship," explains Dale. "It's not unlike the documentaries myself and Janis Cole made where all the characters may seem like antiheroes. In *Hookers on Davie*, Michelle, who is an outrageous drag queen that is half woman, half man, inside is a very warm and wonderful human being. Thematically, I think *Blood & Donuts* is in keeping with the work I've always done, trying to dispel stereotypes."

Dispelling stereotypes is exactly what Dale is doing directing *Blood & Donuts*. Usually considered a "boy's" domain, rarely has a horror film been handed to a woman.

"There's a definite feminist brush stroke throughout the whole piece," agrees Dale, "but it's not written as a feminist project. I think we, as women, do get typecast in

doing womanly kind of things. I was surprised when
Colin [Brunton, executive producer of The Feature Film
Project] came to me with that project. I would expect to
be handed a nice love story or a movie about a mother
and daughter."

Gender was never an issue in deciding who should
direct *Blood & Donuts*, says Brunton. The only real
requirement was that the person be a past Resident of the
Canadian Film Centre.

"I read 160 scripts," explains Brunton, "and I had to
look at all the short films that have been made, there's
over 100 of them now! Weirdly enough, my two favourite short films were *Dead Meat* and *Half-Nelson*, and
Steve Hoban [*Blood & Donuts* producer] produced *Half
-Nelson* and Holly directed *Dead Meat*. She's talented. I
looked at *Dead Meat* and it's got style and it's very funny.
She just seemed ideal for this project. It was very obvious
to me. There were a couple of people I thought about, but
in the end I thought that Holly was the best person for it.
I turned out to be right. *Blood & Donuts* is very funny and
very stylish."

Born into a working class family from Parkdale, Dale
did not have a particularly easy lifestyle. Having left home
at fifteen she, like so many teenagers, learned survival on
the streets of Toronto. "I don't remember why," she
answers when asked how she ended up on Yonge Street.
"I came from a broken home. Boring stuff like that."

Dale, with the help of fellow Yonge Streeters, managed to enroll in film school at Sheridan College where
she changed her major from animation to media arts.

"I wanted to do drama," she remembers, "but I didn't

know what to make a film about. Typical of film school. My teacher said, 'Why don't you make a film about what you know best?' Not knowing what that meant, I thought it was a great idea."

What she knew best was the world of massage parlours, drug-dealing and prostitution. She found in her schoolmate, Vancouver-born Cole, the perfect partner to make the film with.

"We met downtown," says Dale. "We were Yonge Street kids, street kids on Yonge Street. We both came from the same backgrounds. We also grew up being part of the streets. We were attracted to each other because, knowing those worlds and yet also knowing the world of the professional, the world I'm in now, we wanted to show what people are, show more than what's on the surface and break down conceptions and stereotypes. It was also attractive to us to put a human face on people that are on the fringes of society."

Relying on personal experiences to make her first film, Dale tracks down a friend of hers who ran a body-rub parlour and who owed her $300.

"I told him, 'Let me make a film in here.' He said okay," remembers Dale. "So Janis and I wiretapped all the rooms, with the knowledge of the women that worked there, but not the customers, and we made our first 10-minute film. It was in 1975 and a bit ahead of its time."

The bug having bitten, the daring duo (Dale directs, Cole writes) apply for their first Canada Council grant as soon as they're out of school. Once the money comes through they make several shorts, including one about women in Penetang's hospital for the criminally insane, dropping the seed for their first feature, *P4W: Prison for Women.*

Screened at the 1981 Festival of Festivals in Toronto, this film, about inmates of Canada's only federal jail for women convicted of murder, went on to win the 1982 Genie Award for Best Documentary. *P4W* also brought international attention to Dale's and Cole's abilities to convey complicated life stories in simple but determined ways. As the late, great Jay Scott once described them, "they grind their axes until they're shiny."

With renewed confidence, the duo embark on an even more ambitious documentary, *Hookers on Davie*, a "humanistic" look at the lives of prostitutes on a Vancouver street. The filming involved equipping the hookers with radio microphones and holing up in a van across the street, window drapes shrouding the camera. The hookers, meanwhile, never knew when they were being filmed resulting in one of the most dispassionate but natural pics of its kind.

A few years later Dale and Cole decide to share with us their experiences as females in the patriarchal world of filmmaking with *Calling the Shots*, a documentary about women filmmakers in the 1980s.

"We started making films at a time when it was very difficult for women filmmakers. Not that it's easy now," says Dale. "We started in the 1970s when there was no Toronto Women in Film and Television. We've never been embraced by the 'institution' sort of speak. We have had some arm's length help from Studio D, but we have never been Studio D filmmakers or part of the Toronto Film Board scene. We really struggled."

Although she'd been making dramatic shorts for a couple of years, it was as a Resident (they don't like to be called students) at the Canadian Film Centre that Dale got the desire to direct a dramatic feature.

"I did want to start in drama, but I fell in love with documentary," confesses Dale. "I believe that to truly understand real people and real situations, documentaries work better. There's not much of a difference to be a good documentary filmmaker and to be a good dramatic one, you just have to be able understand people. You have to know what buttons to push and when to push them; you have to be sensitive to the needs of the subjects or the actors. There was a grounding in breaking myself in documentary film in terms of theatrics, plus it gave me a great knowledge of on-set tools. You shoot your own films, you write your own sets – all those things that someone else would do in drama."

Dale insists that, even though Cole is not officially involved in *Blood & Donuts*, she has been the major moral force behind it.

"When Colin gave me the script for *Blood & Donuts*, she was my biggest cheerleader to go make it," says Dale. "Somebody else would have said, 'What about our business and our company?' There was none of that. She's come to all the screenings of the film and looked at the rushes. She's been my creative consultant throughout the whole film. Finding people like that is incredibly rare."

The collaboration is far from over. Although Cole is busy writing television scripts and Dale will be going back to directing commercials, their dream project is just around the corner.

"It's a feature drama based on a script that Janis is writing called *Dangerous Offender*," explains Dale. "It's the story of Marlene Moore who was the first person in Canada to be made the Most Dangerous Woman in Canada. We met her when we made *P4W*. Janis has written a wonderful screenplay about her life in prison, about how you can't live in prison and you can't live outside of prison. A beautiful story. Marlene's dead now, she committed suicide. She didn't know how to cope outside prison."

Inquisitive and gracious, with exotic eyes and striking cheekbones, Dale has the self-determined confidence of a person whose road to respect and success has not been easy. When asked if there was ever a moment when she thought it wasn't worth it, she utters a loud sigh.

"Every day Janis and I say, 'Should we quit now or should we give it another few years?', " she says seriously. "As we get older you start to think every film is a big struggle, a lot of hard work. You have to really believe in what you want to do otherwise it's just too much hard work. It's like Sisyphus, y'know, you're pushing that rock up the top of the hill and all of a sudden it rolls down again."

So where does she see herself in thirty years?

"On a beach somewhere," she smiles. "Seriously, thirty years from now I hope I'm still alive. I don't ever want to stop living life because of films. I went through that a couple of years ago. Both Janis and I went through a period of tragedy where a number of very close people to us died and it really made us look at life and realize we were spending all our time on movies. I think there's a balance, and a very wonderful balance, that we both have now. We always take time to enjoy life. Thirty years from now I don't want to find myself stressed out making a film. I want to be making films but I want to also enjoy life."

Amen to that.

Published in Take 1 Magazine, *June 1994.*

FILMOGRAPHY

Born in Toronto, Ontario.

- 1. *Dangerous Offender* (1996)
- 2. *Blood & Donuts* (1995)
- 3. *Dead Meat* (1989)
- 4. *Calling the Shots* (1988)
- 5. *Hookers on Davie* (1984)
- 6. *P4W Prison for Women* (1981)
- 7. *Minimum Charge No Cover* (1978)
- 8. *Thin Line* (1977)
- 9. *Cream Soda* (1976).

ATOM EGOYAN

Felicia's Journey

Dubbed Toronto's darling by the local film community, Atom Egoyan has made this city proud, be it when he's the adoration of film-school helmers at the Cannes and Berlin film festivals, or when he is among his peers as a nominee at the Academy Awards. With his previous film, *The Sweet Hereafter*, still reeling in many film lovers' minds, he's back with another dark tale of death and remembrance, *Felicia's Journey*.

Based on a novel by William Trevor, the movie tells the tale of young Felicia (Elaine Cassidy) who leaves her small village in rural Ireland for Birmingham, England, in search of her lover, the father of her unborn child. Instead she finds Hilditch (Bob Hoskins), a solitary man still obsessed with memories of his famous chef mother, Gala (Arsinée Khanjian). Felicia accepts Hildtich's offer of a warm bed, unaware that she may become another one of his victims.

This is the second script you've adapted from a novel. The Sweet Hereafter was written by Russell Banks.

I wasn't planning to do another adaptation, but then this was presented. I've long toyed with the idea about doing a movie about a child's relationship with a parent who's sort of a celebrity and the fact that their only real contact with that parent would be through this wildly successful program. I never really got it beyond an idea, but when I read this book I saw the possibility of grafting that on the character of the mother. This idea of a person, Hilditch, who lives in complete denial of an aspect of his life and who is in contact with through this ritual which allows him to sustain a relationship that was otherwise really damaging. Sort of this weird nurturing relationship with the mother where they cook food together and eat meals together, yet it's completely deformed. The story just began to grow.

Did you want to do the project immediately?

I read it and my initial reaction was that I didn't really feel any particular desire to film a young woman's escape from rural Ireland. Then I realized that's not what the story's really about. It's his story. There's this incredible contrast between someone with a very pure, simple experience of being expelled and this man who also felt expelled from his garden in a real way. Her garden is this rural, pastoral Irish setting, and his garden is this strange technicolour perversion. And they're both trying to get to this place, and collide. They're both suspended in time. She's sort of living in a 19th century world where she writes letters to the boyfriend and delivering them to the mother who burns them. So contact is lost. And he's living in this hovel but he's very much a monster of our time. And she's also a product of our time. I liked the simplicity. After the structural ambitions of the last film, I was happy to pair it down and just focus on these two characters.

What are the advantages of working with another person's story?

What a really seasoned writer's world does is it gives the opportunity to take something outside of your experience and to interpret it and hopefully arrive at something which surprises you. When I write about my characters, I feel that they are all aspects of me somehow. But when I write Russell Banks or William Trevor, they are definitely outside of my experience. I think those writers definitely have a gift, they're doing something that's quite miraculous which is something I don't do.

You talk about children in this film like you did in your previous one. Has this become a concern since you've become a father?

The notion of what constitutes innocence, what is the nature of parenthood, and the idea of values has always fascinated me. There's this idea of responsibility and who's responsible for what. These ideas in a family that are functioning properly are implicit. But when it becomes dysfunctional suddenly those ideas have to be addressed, and children become perverted and people become panicked when they do things they shouldn't do. That interests me, that point in which male figures reach a panic point in their lives when they realize they're transforming into something else. You go through your adult life without thinking what it is that you can contribute to life, what is the moral thing to do. But when you have a child you have to sit down and question what are the values that you were raised with and if they're actually valid. And sometimes the answers shock you.

Felicia's Journey *also deals with cultural clashes, another recurring theme for you.*

I think being outside of those two cultures I do see them as very different in a way that issues of class and privilege work in England are so different from those of

Ireland. I actually saw in the book an opportunity to explore what history might be. I took notions of history and violence as interesting, the politics of bringing a young child to this destroyed castle and to retell the story of brutality in the force and how this castle was destroyed by that force. There's something ritualized about that and very dangerous about that. The passage that Felicia goes through has to do with everything she's inherited greatly from her father and great-grandmother and all of a sudden she has to arrive on her own sense of what history is. And history is the names of all those women that were killed, and remembering those names becomes her mission and that I found to be a very moving passage. This is a film about the power of memories and the story is affected by those memories, and she chooses in the end to embrace that particular aspect of history.

Did you ever think of setting the film in Canada?

Oh yeah. I thought this would be great in a Canadian setting; I thought Hilditch would be in Victoria, living very comfortably and luring young travelling women. And Felicia would come from a small town in Quebec totally at odds with the stuffiness of Anglophile Victoria. But Icon Production had insisted that the movie be set in Ireland and England.

There was controversy at the Cannes Film Festival when you left suddenly after discovering you didn't win. What happened?

We found out from the publicist what the results were of the awards. We had no reason to stay once we knew we didn't win. It was a very strange festival. I went there telling myself not to get sucked into the "zone" that everyone else is in, but then once you get there you can't help yourself, you can't stop it. You just get into that mode and then you hate yourself for allowing that to happen. I'm glad it's over.

Published in Tandem Magazine, *September 1999.*

FILMOGRAPHY

Born in Cairo, Egypt, on July 19, 1960.

- *Ararat* (2002)
- *The Line* (2000)
- *Felicia's Journey* (1999)
- *The Sweet Hereafter* (1997)
- *A Portrait of Arshile* (1995)
- *Exotica* (1994)
- *Calendar* (1993)
- *Montréal vu par...* (1991)
- *The Adjuster* (1991)
- *Speaking Parts* (1989)
- *Family Viewing* (1987)
- *Men: A Passion Playground* (1985)
- *Next of Kin* (1984)
- *Open House* (1982)
- *Peep Show* (1981)
- *After Grad with Dad* (1980)
- *Howard in Particular* (1979)

ANGELA FEATHERSTONE

200 *Cigarettes*

Most may not be familiar with her name, but Toronto-bred Angela Featherstone is certainly a household face for lovers of highbrow comedies and sitcoms. From "Chloe the Xerox girl" in *Friends* responsible for breaking up Rachel and Ross to Jerry Seinfeld's girlfriend/maid in the last season of *Seinfeld*, to the Adam Sandler's bitchy fiancée in *The Wedding Singer,* Featherstone is slowly but surely making a name for herself in the biz as a comedy actress to be reckoned with, not an easy feat when you're as beautiful as she is.

"I've noticed that few attractive actresses get comedy roles," says Angela. "I've really been studying the comedy thing in the way it is and the way it works, and I noticed that with comedy when I first started going out to auditions I'd never get the jobs that I really wanted because they thought that you can't be pretty and funny at the same time. Of course you can be. There is work, but the really funny roles will be for the ugly bartender, say. That's how I got my first real break in the comedy world. I had gone in for the pilot of a sitcom and I went for the role of this wisecracking bartender chick and they didn't want to see me, but I finally got in and they loved me but they ended up casting somebody else who wasn't really attractive. Later I went to the comedy festival, and word got out that I was really funny. It's a boy's club for the most part, but they let me in. I consider myself really lucky."

Her latest role in Risa Bramon Garcia's *200 Cigarettes* may just give her that thrust upwards she needs. Set in New York's East Village on New Year's Eve 1981, the movie follows around a motley crew of characters who head out to the same loft-party but not before picking up somebody to wake up with the next morning. Featherstone, who plays man-hungry and sexy Caitlyn, is joined by an impressive who's who of Hollywood's up-and-comers: Ben Affleck, Dave Chappelle, Elvis Costello, Guillermo Diaz, Janeane Garofalo, Gaby Hoffman, Jay Mohr, Martha Plimpton, Christina Ricci and Paul Rudd.

"With that kind of cast you can't really say no," smiles Angela when asked what attracted her to the role. "Also hanging around in New York for a week with some of the guys was a lot of fun. I knew Dave Chappelle from *Con Air* and we hang in the same comedy circles, so the fact that he too was in the movie made it more fun."

This scribe remembers hanging around with Featherstone when the then-model lived in T.O., and she never missed a good party. So relating to Caitlyn's sense of desperation in bedding a guy for the night mustn't have been a far stretch.

"Honestly on New Year's Eve, as far as I can remember, I was always a contrarian," laughs Angela. "It was always the night I stayed in and watched TV, but every other night was New Year's Eve. I never liked being pressured into meeting guys. I'd be the kind of person who'd sit in the back of the room in a corner and look for the one weirdo who's sitting on the other side of the room in a corner instead of being out there, like my character in the movie. I'm not really like that."

Raised in Manitoba, then Nova Scotia, Featherstone moved to Toronto in the late-1980s to pursue a career in modeling which landed her on the cover of this country's top fashion magazines. "I don't talk too much about it," says Angela. "I'm known as an actor in Hollywood and not as a model-turned-actor. I want to play a lot of characters, and if I'm known as a model-turned-actor I'd be limited in the range of roles offered me. I wouldn't be able to run around in acid-wash jeans and bad wigs like my character in *The Wedding Singer*."

It's for that reason that Featherstone, after studying acting and unable to land an agent here, left Toronto in 1994 for New York. There she landed a small part in Sam Raimi's *Army of Darkness*, followed by roles in *Con Air, The Zero Effect, Illtown* and *The Wedding Singer*. Yet most people still have a hard time recognizing her.

"I know, that's why my agent is always trying to get me not to wear a wig because people don't know my face," she smiles. "But that's a compliment to me because I don't want to be on the cover of *Vanity Fair* or the latest hot-shot actress for a while and then fade out. I would like to have the option to work for a very long time. I admire somebody like Joan Allen who does so many small parts that are consistently good. If that means wearing different kinds of wigs or crazy make-up and costumes, that's fine with me. I'm not in the business to be successful; I've already been there. As an actor I want to work for a long time."

Featherstone has just finished filming *Take Down*

with Skeet Ulrich and Russel Wong, and is hoping that a sitcom she developed might actually be picked up by a network. Meanwhile she enjoys her new life in La La land.

"It's fun. My best friend from Canada moved in next door and we get together for Canadian nights," she smiles. "The other night Norm Macdonald came and we had Maple Leaf cookies, back-bacon sandwiches and beer."

Published in Tandem Magazine, *February 1999.*

FILMOGRAPHY

Born in Hamilton, Ontario.

- *Constricted* (2003)
- *One Way Out* (2002)
- *Federal Protection* (2002)
- *Pressure* (2002)
- *Soul Survivors* (2001)
- *Rituals and Resolutions* (2000)
- *Ivansxtc* (2000)
- *Skipped Parts* (2000)
- *The Guilty* (1999)
- *Takedown* (1999)
- *200 Cigarettes* (1999)
- *The Wedding Singer* (1998)
- *Zero Effect* (1998)
- *Con Air* (1997)
- *Illtown* (1996)
- *Dark Angel: The Ascent* (1994)
- *Army of Darkness* (1993)

Annie Galipeau

Grey Owl

Heralded by kings and commoners alike, Grey Owl was perhaps the most famous "Indian" in the world and the first person to bring the plight of Canadian endangered beavers to global attention. But Grey Owl, in his forty-eight years of life, was also perhaps one our country's most enigmatic figures.

The life of this great man, and author of the best-selling books *Men of the Last Frontier, Pilgrims of the Wild* and *Tales of an Empty Cabin,* is being immortalized by Sir Richard Attenborough *(Gandhi)* in *Grey Owl,* a movie starring Pierce Brosnan in the title role and Annie Galipeau as Pony, the Iroquois woman who changes his life.

In fact before meeting Pony in 1932, Grey Owl was a respected and self-sufficient trapper who had adjusted to the cruelties of his profession. But after Pony moves in with him and adopts two orphaned baby beavers, Grey Owl falls in love with the small creatures and develops a change of heart in regards to trapping. In order to make a living, Pony convinces her lover to lecture about the endangered animals which leads to worldwide tours and success.

Even though Grey Owl was a household name in Native homes, Annie Galipeau, a pure-blood (mother is one hundred percent Alqonquin and father a Metis) was

unaware of the legend of Grey Owl when Richard Attenborough first auditioned her for the part of Pony.

"Actually my grandfather would talk about Grey Owl
when I was a child but I didn't remember much," says
Galipeau in her heavy French-Canadian accent. "So when
Richard told me that I had the part, I started to learn as
much about him as I could. I read everything, I watched
everything just to be in touch with Grey Owl."

And what she learned was the story of an almost
miraculous transformation. "After he meets Pony he
changes as a man," says the stunning Galipeau. "He
becomes a better human, a good man."

But the most beautiful thing for Galipeau, and for
most Canadian Natives is the story of the "real" Grey
Owl. Only after his death was his true identity revealed.
It turns out that Grey Owl was in fact born Archibald
Stansfield Belaney in Hastings, England. Fascinated at an
early age with North American Indians, he researched as
much as possible on these people until, at the age of
seventeen, he boarded a ship for Canada. Here he moved
to the Temagami district of Ontario, and transformed
himself into an Apache half-breed learning over 200
words of Ojibwa and joining an Ojibway tribe. "The most
beautiful thing about him is that he wanted to be an
Indian," says Galipeau. "He learned everything there was
to learn about Indians, how to walk like an Indian, how
to think like an Indian, and how to talk like an Indian.
That is the greatest compliment to our people."

As for Galipeau, few can say that a shooting delay of
a movie is a good thing. In fact when Attenborough first
auditioned Galipeau for *Grey Owl*, she was little more

than a child. "This was six years ago," says the actress. "It seems that he saw me in *Map of the Human Heart* and wanted to see me. So I go to Montreal with mother, I was fourteen years old, and when he sees me he goes, 'I really don't want to make another Lolita,' and then he said, 'If you were four years older you'd be perfect that role.' "

Luckily for her it took Attenborough four years to get enough financing together to make the film, and one of the first people he called was Galipeau. "So I go to Montreal to meet Richard for the second time, and when he sees me he says, 'Awwww, I can't believe it.,' " laughs Annie. "His eyes were getting bigger and bigger and his smile was getting larger and larger. 'Can you be in California in two weeks?' he asks. Yes. What do I have to do in California? 'You have to do some screen tests. You'll meet Pierce Brosnan.' I was more nervous of meeting Pierce than doing the screen test."

And the rest, as they say, is history. But how did the young actress manage those sultry love scenes with Mr. Bond?

"I was really nervous in the beginning," giggles Annie. "I've never done a love scene, not even a kissing scene, so I said to Pierce, 'I'm not real comfortable doing this. Tell me about the love scene, how it's going to be shot, what I have to do.' And the only answer he gave me was, 'Just be in Pony's skin and everything will be fine.' And he was right. The touching and the kissing and looking in each other's eyes, it all worked out fine."

But *Grey Owl* is not without some controversy. The movie romanticizes this man who dedicated the latter part of his life to saving wildlife, but almost completely ignores some of the ugliest truths about Archie Belaney. There is little mention of his first marriage to Angèle, the Ojibwa girl he married and whom he abandoned along with his infant daughter. And there's no mention about Marie Girard, the Metis woman whom he also abandoned with the baby son who would die of tuberculosis. His second "bigamous" marriage took place in his home of Hastings with his childhood sweetheart Ivy, who would promptly divorce him at news of his infidelities.

The character of Pony is actually based on Gertie, the Iroquois woman Grey Owl would marry in 1926. But Gertie became impatient with Grey Owl's acute alcoholism (it was reported he drank turpentine when he'd run out of liquor) and would leave him in 1935 along with their daughter. Later that same year Archie married "bigamously" Yvonne Perrier who stayed with him long enough to see him shunned by the press due to his alcoholism and violence, and to see him die in 1938.

"Making this movie is a dream come true for Richard," says Galipeau in Attenborough's defense. "Richard met Grey Owl when he was a boy, and I loved hearing Richard talk about him. He was in awe of the man, and I think he wants the viewers to feel the same way. I don't think the other things that Grey Owl did are as important as what he did for the beavers."

On the subject of beavers, what ever happened to those adorable cubs in the movie?

"They were such fantastic animals, just to have them in your hands, to kiss them and to hug them, it was wonderful and they're always screaming and they're always hungry," says Annie. "But they've been returned to the bush. Beavers never lose their animal instincts, ever, so I told Richard that we had to bring them back to woods, and that's what we did. I was very happy for them when they were returned to the bush. They didn't choose to be beaver stars."

Published in Tandem Magazine, *October 1999.*

FILMOGRAPHY

Born in 1979, in Quebec.

- *Grey Owl* (1999)
- *Map of the Human Heart* (1992)

PETER GENTILE

Guy Lombardo: When We Danced

For decades "Auld Lang Syne" has been synonymous with the ringing in of the New Year, but how many of us knew that it is an Italian-Canadian bandleader who brought the unknown Scottish dittie to worldwide attention?

In fact for years Guy Lombardo and His Royal Canadians would play the tune at the stroke of midnight on New Year's Eve from Times Square in New York City, and now with the millennium nearing its end it is only fitting that we remember him in a documentary titled *Guy Lombardo: When We Danced.*

"I thought it would be perfect timing," says producer Peter Gentile. "I remember when I was a kid growing up in Toronto and I couldn't go out New Year's Eve, and I was stuck in front of the television set and the one guy I used watch was Guy Lombardo. My dad used to tell me he's Italian and he's Canadian and I always thought that it was cool that he was in New York doing the New Year's Eve thing."

The Lombardo New Year's Eve Party was the longest running annual special program in radio history. Its first telecast aired in 1954 and when Lombardo performed his final one in 1976, just months before his death, more than 1.5 billion viewers tuned in.

It all began at the turn of the century when a young man named Gaetano Lombardo left his home of Lipiri, a tiny island off the coast of Sicily, to join relatives in London, Ontario. A wannabe musician all his life, Gaetano became a successful tailor in London, and while at the YMCA Squire he played the odd musical instrument. "He was not a bad musician but he wasn't schooled," says Gentile. "But as he started his own family it became very important for him that his kids learn music. He used to tell his kids all the time, 'Learn music. It's a light load to carry.' "

His four sons, Guy, Carmen, Liebert and Victor, and two daughters, Rosemarie and Elaine, were taught music by Maestro Venuto, whom Gaetano flew in from Italy. And when Venuto returned home, the father took over the role as taskmaster making his kids practice before (from 8 a.m. to 9 a.m.) and after school (from 4 p.m. to 6.p.m.).

The discipline paid off. The children's mother got them to play at the Italian social clubs in and around the London, Ontario area soon gaining popularity. The band was formed in 1916 and Guy, being the eldest, became the leader with billing under his name with brothers Liebert and Carmen as equal partners in the business. The Guy Lombardo and His Royal Canadians moved to Cleveland in 1927, where they got regular radio airplay. They were solidly mainstream, occasionally dabbling in light classical ("Tales from the Vienna Woods") or risking something as wild as swing. A saxophone-heavy sound was the signature of the Royal Canadians, used to humorous effect in one of their biggest hits, "Boo Hoo."

"He wasn't very respected in music circles," says Gentile. "There was this idea that he was out of step with society, and he was never on the cutting edge of what was happening in music. He was a bit of a caricature of himself and to try and get past that, to get to what the guy was really like, was tough because it was quite a while ago and a lot of people aren't around anymore."

For over forty years, Guy Lombardo and his orchestra kept up a steady string of engagements and recordings, with most of the hits coming in the 1930s and 1940s. Although his music was entirely conventional, Lombardo stood by his father's dictum "as long as there's a beat."

"Their key thing was to make people happy and they were looked down upon by the jazz community because jazz is an individualistic kind of genre," explains Gentile. "They got a lot of shots taken at them because of that. But his line was 'nobody likes us but our fans' and they had tons of them. A band that played that long together and that was that successful sold close to 300 million records. They were huge."

Perhaps the secret behind Guy Lombardo's success is the miraculous fact that the band stayed together for nearly fifty years in its original incarnation. The brothers were very close, and the first thing Guy did with his money was buy a house for his parents in Connecticut so they could be close to their children.

"It's unbelievable that they stayed together that long," says Gentile. "The band ended up being this extended family and he treated the band very, very well. He paid the band members more than what was generally paid, more than the Dorseys or Glenn Miller's band members. There was this loyalty."

But there's always a dark cloud, and that happened to

be youngest brother Victor, the only Lombardo who wasn't an equal member in band. "He was an odd cat that Victor," says Gentile whose previous documentary was based on the life of Gilles Villeneuve. "He had his own band and he was always off doing his own thing and losing money. So the father told Guy to put him in the band and get him out of London, so he'd straighten out."

Today all the Lombardo brothers are gone with aging sisters Rosemarie and Eileen living quiet lives in the U.S. And while watching the terrific *Guy Lombardo: When We Danced*, one can't help shake a sad sense of melancholy, similar to the kind one feels when listening to "Auld Lang Syne."

"I know exactly how you feel," says Gentile. "It's a time in history that no longer exists, a time when a handshake was a handshake and you didn't need a contract. That's what's sad about it. That's why the New Year's Eve song is fitting. It's about remembering the guy who gave us this song about remembering well, let's remember him because he's really been forgotten."

Published in Tandem Magazine, *May 1999.*

FRANÇOIS GIRARD

The Red Violin

Shot in five languages, in five countries and over the span
of three centuries, François Girard's *The Red Violin* is the
most expensive movie in Canadian history. A co-produc-
tion with Italy's Mikado, the movie begins in 17th-cen-
tury Cremona where master violinmaker Nicolo Bussotti
(Carlo Cecchi) creates his latest masterpiece on the eve of
a disaster. The violin is then brought to an Austrian
monastery landing in the hands of a child prodigy (Christoph Koncz). Stolen by Gypsies, the violin travels to
England where it's bought by a troubled violinist, ending
up in China and, finally, in modern-day Montreal.

Why embark on such an ambitious project?
I think you would have to be a bit crazy to embark on
a project like this. It doesn't start with wanting to do
something in five languages, wanting to do a complicated
movie, or wanting a bigger budget. It starts with me
wanting to tell this story about the life of the violin, and
soon after you realize the implications of that. It then
becomes a journey through time, a journey through different countries, then it goes around the world, five
languages, and the project becomes more expensive. All
those things came later and you learn to deal with the
consequences. It begins with a dream that you have and
that you fight for.

Where did the idea come from?

The truth is it comes from everything I've done be-fore. When you make a movie like *The Red Violin* it's the sum of everything you've done before. You re-digest your own experiences into a movie. Niv [Fichman, producer], Don [McKellar, screenwriter) and I wanted to work to-gether again and I was offered many music films and I was resisting them. Suddenly I had this idea that was perfect for us to do together. Niv is a great traveler, it's a love that we share, and he's also interested in different cultures as Don is. We found in *The Red Violin* a common interest, a common passion for the different things that were repre-sented.

Are any of the episodes based on true stories?

No, the whole thing is fictitious, but of course I'm inspired by thousands of facts and stories. We nourished the writing with quite intensive research on all the violin stories such as stolen violins, fake violins, lost violins. The backgrounds of these stories we didn't create, so we connected that with history but never on a first basis. In order to keep the movie intimate, because we spent so little time on the characters, we had to concentrate more on the stories than the historical backgrounds.

What was it like working in Cremona, the home of Stradivari?

I went to Cremona many times, the first time soon after I decided to make this, even before starting the research. I went there to see the people, see the violin-making schools, see the little shops, meet the violinmak-ers just to get a sense of what the town's about. I just screened them the film.

How was it?

It was great fun. Cremona is still known for its violins, and a lot of the people sitting in the room had something to do with violins. There are 150 shops in Cremona that deal with violins. Having them sit through the film was a bit like showing them what happens to their instruments after they leave the shop. They loved it.

You hired some of them as extras.

Yes, anybody who had to do anything with a violin, like hold it, I felt the best people to do that would have to be the actual experts. It's those little things that can drive you crazy; if I were an actor I would have to research that, I would have to learn how to hold that wood. Some of the actors, for example, had to learn how to hold it, how to turn it, how to look at it. It was very complicated. So there was this workshop scene in Cremona where the violinmakers are working, and they were real violinmakers. They offered authenticity without too much effort.

And the little Austrian boy, Christoph Koncz?

He is an incredible violinist. On top of everything he actually composed that character. He's strong, very Germanic, blue eyes, glasses and we had to make him frail, sick and fragile.

But he's not an actor. He became an actor. We looked at all the Vienna prodigies for the one that would do the part. We looked at a lot of boys, and when he walked into the room and grabbed the violin, I got goosebumps because he was so intense. He transformed as soon as he got the violin in his hands. It was very emotional. I felt that if he can deliver such emotions with that instrument, he can probably transport that in his acting. I went for the very best violinist because we needed the best, and I assumed it also meant very smart and a great learner, all the qualities needed to be a good actor. But Jason Flemyng, who plays the British violinist, was a real actor.

That was the opposite process. In that case we thought the best thing to do was use the best actor. But adjusting the music was hard, and I'm proud of the tricks I played. It was hard work for Jason, four months of violin lessons, then violinist Joshua Bell came in with more lessons. The concert sequence was shot with him alone, and it was believable, but the close-up was tight so you see the elbows, but the elbows were tied to two other players, Joshua on his left hand, and another violinist doing the bowing. So these players had to be in perfect sync. I called that the octopus.

Which was the hardest shoot?

Montreal. It was the toughest to write and the toughest to shoot. It had to do with the double-resolution of the sequence, and that put me and Don and the actors in a very difficult situation. We were always walking on a thin line, and nothing was clear. We always had to do two things at the same time.

And the most pleasurable shoot?

Italy, because of the great crew and great food. Things are looser but in the end they always fall into place. It's dancing but it's a beautiful dance. We had a lot of fun.

Published in Tandem Magazine, *November 1998.*

FILMOGRAPHY

Born in 1963, in St-Felicien, Quebec.

- *The Red Violin* (1998)
- *Thirty Two Short Films About Glenn Gould* (1993)
- *Cargo* (1990)

MARY JANE GOMES

Angel in a Cage

While attending a symposium on Caribbean film in Ohio several months ago, Canadian director Mary Jane Gomes was approached by a young woman from the southern United States who said, "That was my mother, and that was my grandmother."

She was referring to Carmina, the heroine in Gomes' debut feature film *Angel in a Cage*, an intimate tale set in Trinidad in the 1930s.

"I had many comments that evening but her's was the one that really touched my heart," remembers Gomes.

You see, *Angel in a Cage* is the story of Gomes' grandparents, well, kinda, Portuguese colonialists producing Madeira wine in a small Trinidadian village.

"It's actually set in my grandparents' milieu. There are some family anecdotes and some history there, but it is fictitious in the sense that I don't know what really happened then," explains Gomes. "I went to the Canadian Film Centre in its inaugural year and we were really encouraged to go back to our roots so that we would be writing in a world that was familiar to us even though I was going farther back to the time of my grandparents in Trinidad. I grew up in Trinidad, and so the whole milieu, the language of the film and the feeling of time and place come out of my childhood. It is not factually my grandmother's story but it certainly fed in the circumstances around her life close to when she died."

And a fascinating story it is. This scribe, for example, was unfamiliar with the fact that many Portuguese living in Madeira were brought to Trinidad as indentured labourers once slavery was finally abolished. Such was the case for Gomes' great-grandparents who were Madeira winemakers living on the tropical island.

"It's interesting that the Portuguese learned their English in the streets of Trinidad and ended up staying and opening little shops in little rural villages," says Gomes. "What happened was that they were never accepted as white in the colonial world and they were obviously not black but they became this sort of colonialists of the rural villages and their lives had a closer interface with the black communities than the people of other racial origins who were white."

For Gomes the filmmaker, who was born in Guyana and lived in Trinidad until moving to Canada at the age of five, this caused no few problems. "In the making of this film I would be sent off to see the mainstream people and they would look at the language of the film and say, 'No, no, you have to go to the cultural sector,' and I would go to the cultural sector and they would look at my skin and say, 'No, no, no, no.' So in a way my grandparents' lives fell between those cracks and in pursuing a story that is along the same cultural division, I faced the same problems in the way of making my work that they faced in their daily lives."

That isolation and falling between the cracks is clearly reflected in *Angel in a Cage*, the story of XAV (Tony

Nardi), his sickly wife Carmina (Maurina Gomes, the director's sister) and his disenchanted brother Bosie (Christopher Pinheiro), who all long for their faraway home and a better future. And unlike the other colonialists, explains Gomes, the relationship between the Portuguese and the Trinidadians was much more convivial.

"The colour didn't matter," she insists. "The Caribbeans had a very different relationship with the Europeans than other colonies did. It's maybe not always the same from family to family but it's definitely that relationship that is portrayed in the film."

What's particularly intriguing about *Angel in a Cage* is its stringent use of the island patois. "I wrote that patois," says proudly Gomes. "When I went to the Film Centre our first writing instructor sat us down one evening and said, 'Become five years old and walk into a room and stay there. Then come back the next day and write two pages of a screenplay.' Well, I came back with this language. It was my first language that I knew and that I didn't realize I knew. It was locked inside of me from the age of five. The Trinidadian language is very much an English patois, Trinidadians wouldn't say, 'It's raining outside,' they'd say, 'Rain falling.' It's very poetic."

Before venturing into filmmaking, Gomes was an alternative journalist who wrote and researched for the liberation of southern Africa for at least decade, an interest she credits directly to her upbringing in the Caribbean. "I've always had this sense of discerning judgement that has been handed down to me and that has made me interested in the politics of what was going on in those places," she confirms. "It's been a real central part of my life. The first money I made when I was a student in Canada was to buy a plane ticket back to Trinidad. And that was the start of it."

Angel in a Cage is the first of a trilogy of semi-biographical movies dealing with life in Madeira and the Caribbean (the next two will be *The House of Cousins* and *In the Land of the Hummingbirds*), so one wonders what the actual inspiration for these stories thinks about the project.

"My mother is really, really moved," says Gomes. "It's interesting because she and my father knew that world intimately. My mother lost her mother at a very, very young age and as time goes by she says she misses her more. She can't stop watching the movie. It's very powerful for her. It's very wonderful for them to feel that it's authentic."

Published in Word Magazine, *June 1999.*

FILMOGRAPHY

Born in Guyana.

- *Angel in a Cage* (1999)

LAURA HARRIS

Kitchen Party

In the U.S. it was Richard Linklater who re-invented the darkly comic filmic look at suburban dysfunction (*Dazed and Confused, Suburbia*). In Canada, that accolade goes to Gary Burns, the creator of *The Suburbanators* (1995) and the newly released *Kitchen Party*.

Here we're in a middle-class Vancouver suburb where Scott (Scott Speedman) is taking advantage of his parents' absence to have a few friends over for a party on the eve of his leave for university. The hitch? There must be absolutely no trace of a party taking place by the time Mom and Dad get home from their dinner party. So Scott tries to confine the party to the kitchen, but when you combine teenage libidos with alcohol, we all know what the outcome is.

"I didn't grow up in the suburbs, but I can certainly relate to these kids," says Laura Harris who plays Tammy, the only cool girl at the party who sees right through the group's frustrated demeanors. "I grew up in the country and where I went to school there were no boys and I didn't party very much. Had I been in that sort of situation like the kids in *Kitchen Party,* I would've felt equally as alienated or possibly even bored, as Tammy was. Nothing much interesting was directed in her way. She wasn't that involved as she found her own amusement, as I'm sure I would've as well. But the film did give me an insight into suburbia and the complete insanity that ensues with extreme boredom. And maybe a few drinks."

Harris confesses, however, some puzzlement at the characters' age group. Having just exited her teen years when she worked on *Kitchen Party*, she discovered on the set that the storyline relates more to the older generation than to her own.

"I've never been to a 'kitchen party,' but I'm probably the only person that hasn't been," she says online from her hotel room in Prague where she's filming Ken Berris' *The Manor*. "Especially people who were in that movie, the cast, and even the crew. People who were a lot older, in their twenties really remember being in kitchen parties, or ending up in a kitchen at the end of the night. That's when all the interesting stuff was going on. But I don't recall anyone not ever being allowed into any other room, certainly there's always one room blocked off. But the whole house? That's a little anal, I think."

Burns insists that although the script isn't based on his life, it is loosely based on people he grew up with.

"He's actually been to a party where someone had to vacuum a symmetrical pattern in their living room so that the parents wouldn't find out," laughs Harris. "He experienced suburbia in all its heinous glory. I've been really amazed at how much this film really caters to an older audience than the kids who are actually in it. Like the people who are Gary's age and who remember these kind of things, or my sisters and brothers who are in their late twenties. They can really identify with it."

While Harris may long for missed experiences, she has nothing to envy others in her profession. Only twenty-one, the Vancouverite began her career at the age of five appearing in television shows and low-budget movies until landing her first ever feature-film lead in Rene Daalders' *Habitat* (1992), alongside Balthazar Getty and Kenneth Welsh. She then went on to co-star in Mark Sawyer's *Skyscraper* next to Taylor Nichols (*Metropolitan, Barcelona*).

"They're not big films, only small independent features with names," says Harris modestly. "But in the scheme of American films, they're considered very small and independent."

While *Kitchen Party* has garnered critical acclaim at film festivals around the world, it's *Suicide Kings* that will most likely thrust young Harris into the limelight. Directed by Peter O'Fallon, the film focuses on a group of friends (played by Henry Thomas, Sean Patrick Flanery and John Galecki) who kidnap a crime boss (Christopher Walken) after one of the guys' sister (Harris), who's also the girlfriend of another, is kidnapped.

"Getting the role was pure luck," says Harris. "When I first got down to Los Angeles after filming *Kitchen Party*, I had an audition for another film, and they said I was too young but that I was perfect for this other one and to please go down and audition for that. And they hired me."

Suicide Kings, which also stars a hilarious Denis Leary as Walken's henchman, screened at the Toronto International Film Festival last year to horrid reviews.

"It's completely re-cut," assures me Harris of the new version. "The movie that you saw at the Festival, and I saw that too, had a completely different ending and it's a different movie. Happily so. I'm much happier with the new ending than the old one."

Was Harris intimidated at all in sharing the set with a group of relative screen stars?

"Not intimated or worried, but perhaps nervous," she says. "I want to be a good part of something that's happening. I want to contribute in a good way, that they're happy that they hired me. I think when you're really young there's a perception that you have of the whole business that's hard to let go of. You don't buy into the whole notion of stars being non-human. The business is the business, it's not some far away unreachable and untouchable thing. It's work, it's a career, it's creation. But it's not terrifying, it's not intimidating at all."

What of her next film, *Just the Ticket*, starring Andy Garcia and Andie MacDowell? She can't convince me that Garcia didn't make her a wee bit nervous.

"He's amazing, he's really amazing," she says. "He was remarkable in every way to me. He's so sexy and so beautiful and generous and his family is there all the time on the set. I play a street kid, his sidekick I guess, drugged and three months pregnant. It's a true story about New York's best ticket scalper during the time the Pope came to town. It's really interesting. The guy who's story it is was on set, and he was really happy with my character who was a real girl but who actually ended up dying. I don't think she dies in the movie because it borders on a romantic comedy."

While Garcia and the Suicide pack are cool enough, what Harris is really itching to talk about is *The Manor*, a British dark comedy murder mystery featuring a remarkable mostly female cast of Greta Scacchi, Gabrielle Anwar, Fay Masterson and Harris in one of the leads.

"It's really great and everyone is so into," says an excited Harris. "The script is very worthy, it's completely character driven. Scenes go on for pages and pages and pages, and they're enthralling scenes to read never mind watch when you get some really strong women together to start talking it out. I'm having the time of my life."

And it's just beginning.

Published in Access Magazine, *March 1998.*

FILMOGRAPHY

Born November 20, 1976, in Vancouver, British Columbia.

- *A Mighty Wind* (2002)
- *Come Together* (2001)
- *Going Greek* (2001)
- *The Calling* (2000)
- *The Highwayman* (1999)
- *Just the Ticket* (1999)
- *The Manor* (1999)
- *The Faculty* (1998)
- *Kitchen Party* (1997)
- *Suicide Kings* (1997)
- *Habitat* (1997)
- *Stay Tuned* (1992)

BRUCE MCDONALD

Dance Me Outside

Where would one find a frustrated barber travelling from Sudbury to St. Louis with a corpse on his car's roof? Where would one find a timid assistant travelling Northern Ontario in search of a wayward rock'n'roll band only to find an aspiring serial killer and The Ramones? In Bruce McDonald's lovely and quirky mind, that's where.

Canada's most beloved outlaw filmmaker has brought us through some pretty demented territory with his first two features, *Roadkill* and *Highway 61*. With his new film, *Dance Me Outside* the Toronto native has pulled the reins on his runaway imagination. Instead of a road movie chock-full of freakish characters comes the charming story of two teenage boys and their lives on the Kidabanesee reservation.

Based on short stories by W.P. Kinsella *(Shoeless Joe)*, *Dance Me Outside* is a fast-paced, thoroughly enjoyable movie featuring an incredibly talented cast of virtual unknowns. Funny, tragic and never predictable, this film may actually thrust McDonald out of the art houses and into the first-run.

What do you think about Dance Me Outside *being billed as* Bill and Ted on the Reservation?

I like it. I first got involved in this about three years ago and I remember the first thing I decided was to try and make a teenage movie rather than try to position it as some kind of movie about Native life. It's that, anyway, so let's try and make this about two guys, Frank and Silas, who are like any guy teen: there's the active one and there's the crafty one.

But a lot more serious.

Yeah. They have their little lingo, although not as goofy, and they live on a reservation surrounded by tragedy and misery. There have been enough movies and documentaries and books made about that. We tried to show the other side of the reserve, play up the humour and try to make people fall in love with these characters, but also get a very small sense of some of the things they have to deal with.

Why make this film?

I've done two road movies and really both out of the same idea. At the Toronto Film Festival, after we screened *Highway 61*, Norman Jewison saw the film and liked it and he had been trying to develop this project for a long time with different writers and the intention of directing it. He'd given it his shot and wasn't quite sure where to take it, so he decided to give this new filmmaker a shot with it. I knew as much about Indians as anybody before I got this script. It took me a few months to just decide if this was something I wanted to do. What attracted me to the project was what happens to a group of teenagers when one of their friends is killed. It had more of a story than I had ever dealt with before.

Your cast is fantastic.

I'm proud of the cast. It was a great experience. I fell in love with these actors. Usually I work with people I know. I had no history with these actors, they were

younger than me with little or no experience. It was fun
making it. Having these eighteen-nineteen year-old actors
around was great. They were very excited about the fact
they were making this movie and because they were
making a movie where they didn't have to wear a loin-
cloth, they didn't have to shoot a bow and arrow, and
they didn't have to paddle a canoe. They were playing
characters, and they thought that was fantastic. They
loved the fact that they could wear Metallica T-shirts and
they could drive a car and kiss girls.

*Was there a conflict you being white making a film
about Natives?*

Not really. The reserves that we shot at are up near
Parry Sound on Parry Island. We met with the two Chiefs,
and they thought it was very good for the community
because we would hire some of the kids in the cast and
people for our crew. I think there are advantages to
making a film about a place you don't really have a history
with because you see things in a slightly different way. It's
up to that person to treat it with respect. When we went
up to the reserve, being white guys and, even more than
that, being city folk, we were these potential Toronto
assholes coming up to shoot a film. Very quickly people
realized we're from Toronto but we're not assholes. People shoot the term around, Appropriation of Culture, but
I've yet to hear a clear definition of that. My thinking is,
if you consider yourself an artist or a creative person,
that's what you do. You take this voice, that voice and you
add your own personality and experiences and it becomes
something new.

How does your film differ from Kinsella's book?

Kinsella's book is a bit dated. We take two basic stories from it, one called *Dance Me Outside* and one called *Ilianna Comes Home*, which are the two basic threads in the movie: the revenge story against the killer, and the triangle of old boyfriend and couple trying to have a kid. Kinsella's stories operate on a kind of revenge motive, generally. For example, the white lawyer character in the book is portrayed as a complete buffoon that others don't really like, whereas in the movie we tried to change that resolution a little bit where the kids actually have a good time with him, they like him. We humanized things more.

What did Kinsella think about the film?

He showed up at the Vancouver screening. I've never met the guy, but I've been told he's kind of opinionated. He was a little ticked off because he had to pay to see the movie, so he said, "My stories move at lightning speed and I don't think the film matches the pace of my stories." Other than that he really liked the actors. Mostly, he was going on about money, and he was whining about how much he got paid for his story. Kinsella was the highest-paid person on this entire production. He got much more than I did or the producers or Norman or the actors.

What was the hardest thing about making Dance Me Outside?

Getting a script. It went through so many different people. We were trying to remain true to the spirit of Kinsella, the humorous sense of danger, of tragedy. The problem with the book was it's all short stories and no one story can really carry the whole thing so we had to invent this whole other kind of structure of characters in between that. Suddenly it doesn't become the book anymore but something completely different. The previous scripts were either too Hollywood or too plot heavy by using too many stories in the book.

What was the best thing about making Dance Me Outside?

Being up there. It was grueling during the day, but we were staying in these great cabins with fireplaces. It changed our perception about the land, it changed our lives. Even the people on the reserve learned from us. We ripped down stereotypes on both sides.

The soundtrack to the film is pretty awesome as well.

The first time I went to a reserve, the thing that really struck me was the music. They're either huge country-and-western fans, or they're heavy into hardcore like Metallica, Megadeath. I thought it was hilarious. It's what it's all about, this cultural smash-up.

How did this experience affect you personally?

Half-way through the shoot, the Chief, Roger, invited the crew for a pipe ceremony. It was basically this guy talking for a couple of hours. The things he talked about, the kindness, the casualness just seemed very, very right. After the ceremony Roger drew on this big pipe full of tobacco. After he finished, he put the pipe down and lit a cigarette. I looked at him and liked that. Tobacco is a sacred thing, a spiritual thing. The whole idea of tobacco is you light it and the smoke connects you with the creator, it goes off and that's your lifeline to your creator. A few weeks later, at 6 a.m., I was getting out of my little cabin and things were going pretty good. I'm by myself on my way to the truck to go to the set, and I stop and I take a little piece of my cigarette and bury it in the ground and I say a little prayer out loud, like "Hey, it's really great to be here." I've never done anything like that before. I really loved that practical nature of their spirituality: this is the land we live on, we respect it, this is our mother and father is the guy you talk to with the smoke signals. After I did that I stood up and everything felt a little bit different, more friendly. It was a really interesting moment. It had a profound impact on me.

Published in Scene Magazine, *June 1994.*

FILMOGRAPHY

Born on May 28 1959, in Kingston, Ontario.

- *Picture Claire* (2001)
- *Pontypool Changes Everything* (2000)
- *Elimination Dance* (1998)
- *Hard Core Logo* (1996)
- *Dance Me Outside* (1994)
- *Highway 61* (1991)
- *Roadkill* (1989)
- *Knock! Knock!* (1985)
- *Let Me See . . .* (1982)

MIKE MYERS

Austin Powers

"C'mon, baby, let's do it," says Mike Myers in an English cockney accent that lands his spit on the wall behind me. He wants to test my knowledge of 1960s' British hip euphemisms. I'm game. I used to watch *The Avengers* and *Monty Python's Flying Circus*. Piece of cake.

"Shag?" he asks.

Sex.

"Behave?"

Stop touching. Keep your hands to yourself.

"Fab?"

Nice style.

"Randy?"

Horny.

"Choppers?"

Teeth. Bad teeth.

"Saucy?"

Cheeky.

"Cheeky?"

Saucy.

"Groovy, baby," he smiles and gives me a high five.

Myers just can't seem to get out of his Austin Powers mode, but then why should he? Of all the characters he has embodied during his comic career, the swinging 1960's secret agent/fashion photographer/rock star is by far the most fun and colourful. But for Myers it is all second nature. In all the routines he creates, there is always an element of his personal life. Wayne Campbell, for example, the excellent host of *Wayne's World*, is inspired by the buddies he used to hang with in Scarborough, Ontario; Simon, the hyper little boy in the bathtub, is a recreation of his own naughty childhood antics; and Angus, from in *All Things Scottish*, is derived from his horsing around with his dad and brother when he was a child.

"Yeah, my family was pretty crazy," he laughs. "They moved to Canada in 1956 from Liverpool and I grew up in a very English household. My relatives in Liverpool assumed that we were living in an outback and they would send us clothes and food and stuff like if we were roughing it in the bush."

Consequently Myers would receive packages with genuine Beatle boots and Beatle suits, as well as several Nehru jackets that were fashionable in the late 1960s.

"My relatives were very into the Beatles, and I thought I was related to the Beatles growing up, because who talks like that? Nobody except my parents so obviously I'm related," jokes Myers. "My brother, Paul, had kind of a weird separation thing because he thought that my dad was John Lennon for a number of years."

His father, who passed away several years ago, was so obsessed with all things British remembers Myers, that he would wake his sons up in the middle of the night to watch a Peter Sellers or a Peter Cook and Dudley Moore movie.

"I would often miss my first period of school," smiles Myers.

It is no wonder that Myers would develop this love-love relationship with all things British, the culmination of which led him to make a James Bond spoof, *Austin Powers: International Man of Mystery*, about a 1960s secret agent cryogenically frozen and then melted in 1997 to fight the dangerous Dr. Evil.

"I was driving home from a hockey practice and I heard 'The Look of Love' on the radio which is a great, great song," explains Myers on how the idea for Austin Powers first struck him. "Burt Bacharach is awesome, a god. Everything that implied from 'The Look of Love' was 1960s. He wrote that for Ursula Andress and having seen her, she is the look of love, and still is a crazingly sexy woman, outrageously sexy individual. So I started talking in this swinger voice when I got home: 'Hello, baby. How are you, darling?' It made my wife laugh. Eventually she said, 'OK, why don't you just stop and write it down.' And so I wrote it down."

Myers admits that most of his work is a collaborative effort. He credits much of his success to *Wayne's World* co-star Dana Carvey for the many invaluable tips in surviving a business not particularly kind towards comedians.

"One of the things that I learned from Dana was that you can have comedy on a set," he says. "When we would shoot masters, he would have a very obscene picture of my head pasted on his forehead. I would just break out laughing, and so would the crew. Crews never laugh at the end of takes. Even on *Saturday Night Live* crews don't laugh which is disconcerting. But when Dana and I were making the *Wayne's World* movies, it was always a lot of fun."

Which brings us to the next question. Is *Wayne's World* dead, or can we expect a third installation about the partying duo?

"It's certainly not dead, but it's hard for us," says Myers. "Dana has kids and lives in San Francisco, Lorne [Michaels, producer] has kids and lives in New York, and I have dogs and live in Los Angeles. It's hard to get us all in the same room. Just to hang out with Dana we have to get our books out and figure out when he can get a nanny. I saw him at New Year's which was a treat because he's hilarious. He's one of those great guys who is not only funny when he performs but funny in life."

Born and raised in Scarborough, a suburb of Toronto, Myers always had a knack for comedy. He was so confident, in fact, that the day he graduated from high school he also auditioned and was accepted into The Second City comedy troupe in Toronto. This led to his own comedy act, Mullarkey and Myers, which would bring him to London, England, where he would form The Comedy Store Players.

After returning to Toronto, Myers would join The Second City in Chicago, and soon after was recruited to join the cast of *Saturday Night Live* for which he would win an Emmy Award for Best Writing. In the seven years that Myers was a member of *SNL*, he would create a slew of classic and hilarious characters such as Pat Arnold, in Bill Swerski's Super Fans, Dieter, host of Sprockets, Steve Lawrence, in The Sinatra Group, Lothar of the Hill People, Marcello, in Il Cantore and La Cantora, Phillip, the Hyper-Hypo, Linda Richman, host of Coffee Talk, and Handsome Man, Lank Thompson. Aside for the two

Wayne's World movies, he also starred in *So I Married an Axe Murderer.*

Myers recently also branched out into rock'n'roll with recording pals Susanna Hoffs and Matthew Sweet.

"We always threatened to put a band together," says Myers. "So we did a few gigs around town, then we did a couple of gigs at the Viper Room. They liked us so much that they asked us to be the house band. They asked us to play every first Friday and every Monday of the month, and we played a couple of times but we all got busy with other stuff. Too bad. It was fun."

Although he has made his home on the west coast, Myers still admits to missing Toronto and his family. (His mother still lives in Scarborough; his brother, Paul, recently moved to San Francisco.)

"Toronto is always home," he smiles. "There's a certain attitude here that doesn't exist anywhere else in the world. Last night, for example, I went out with my best friend and we went to a bar and five guys came up to talk to us, and one of the guys went, 'Hey, he's with his best friend. Leave him alone.' That's when I thought I'm home; people are very respectful and nice in Toronto. I was on the subway the last time I was here, and this guy came up to me and out of the blue said, 'Hey, hear about the Dougie trade?', and I go, 'Yeah yeah.' I really miss it."

Published in Access Magazine, *June 1997.*

The Spy Who Shagged Me

What does the man, swinging photographer by day, International Man of Mystery by night, do when his "mojo" is stolen from him by arch nemesis Dr. Evil? Such is the new mission by Austin Powers who, in the sequel *The Spy Who Shagged Me*, must travel back to 1969 to recoup his "libido."

Torontonian Mike Myers, the creator and star of the Austin Powers movies, talked about the movie and his career from his office on Los Angeles.

What is the strangest place where somebody walked up to you and said, "Yeah, baby?"

The men's room in Maple Leaf Gardens and it was a very odd sensation to be urinating at the time. But it was very nice.

Are you flattered that the character you've created has had such an impact?

You've got to think of it from my perspective. I grew up in Toronto as a big fan of *Saturday Night Live*. You never actually think you're going to get to do it. Then you write these things and it's weird. It's weird just to be an employed actor. So it's strange to have a total stranger come up and mimic you. It's weird but very flattering.

Did you have any misgivings about doing sequel?

I couldn't wait to do it. But I had two conditions: one, it had to be directed by Jay Roach, and two, it had to be a funnier script than the first film. Jay had just done a sort of serious, but not serious, serious movie [*Alaska*], and I'd done *54*, and this strange Irish movie [*Pete's Meteor*], and then I felt it was time to just have some fun. We had a great time. If somebody told me that contractually every other movie I had to make had to be an Austin Powers movie I'd be very happy.

There's a good possibility of that, like James Bond movies.

Who knows. I took a year and a half off from show business and one of the big things that occurred to me is that you shouldn't make any plans. I really literally don't make any plans. But as a sort of form I would want to do a sort of Pink Panther/James Bond thing, because there's always a new case and that's what's so much fun about it. If it should happen again I would feel happy to do it.

Did you ever think of an Austin Powers television series?

There's an animation series on HBO that'll probably be out in about a year. The reason that I'm interested in doing that is when you write a script you always have at least another script's worth of material that didn't make it in, and the way I'm looking at this animated series of thirteen half-hour shows is that it will be sort of a land of lost toys, jokes that didn't make it anywhere else. It's hard. When you're on *Saturday Night Live* for six years and generating so much material and you just don't have anywhere to put it, it's like a little *jokus interruptus*.

What's the recurring scenario of the Austin Powers movies?

The same as in the James Bond movies. You see him finishing his last mission; then he's given his new mission; he meets with his mentor figure who gives him a special amulet; he crosses over the threshold to an exotic locale where he meets two girls, one of them is a protector, one is the destroyer; then he's taken to the legitimate face of the evil empire and he changes his identity and infiltrates; then two assassins come, on one, he uses his secret amulet, the second, he uses whatever instrument that they have against themselves; then he's taken prisoner and left for dead, and he's put into an easy escapable death situation in which the bad guy never actually checks; then he and the girl escape; rally, reattack again, using superior numbers in forces; they overcome the guy but the guy escapes; then they end up in a raft. That's the movie. So to that extent it's a noble and finite structure. Then we just insert the jokes.

But when you're spoofing a spoof, where do you go?

That's interesting. Gene Siskel said that *Austin Powers* was a tribute movie and not a spoof movie, and that's the spirit in which we came to this. Jay taught film and I always loved movies and it really is a tribute movie. One of the big influences on this movie is *Casino Royale* which in itself was a spoof of a Bond movie.

Although you live in Los Angeles, you keep mentioning in the press how much you love Canada. Why?

I think Canada is the greatest country in the world. It's a very safe country. We never tried to become a melting pot, we're a salad bowl. We have a Ministry of Multiculturalism in Canada. People come from around the world from every ethnicity and it seems that everybody gets along. That is great. I don't know where it exists in anywhere else in the world.

Published in Access Magazine, *June 1999.*

FILMOGRAPHY

Born May 25 1963, in Scarborough, Ontario.

- *The Cat in the Hat* (2003)
- *Austin Powers in Goldmember*(2002)
- *A View from the Top* (2003)
- *Shrek* (Voice, 2001)
- *Mystery, Alaska* (1999)
- *Austin Powers: The Spy Who Shagged Me* (1999)
- *Nobody Knows Anything* (1999)
- *The Thin Pink Line* (1998)
- *Pete's Meteor* (1998)
- *54* (1998)
- *Austin Powers: International Man of Mystery* (1997)
- *Wayne's World 2* (1993)
- *So I Married an Axe Murderer* (1993)
- *Wayne's World* (1992)
- *Elvis Stories* (1989)

TONY NARDI

Bonanno: A Godfather's Story

Tony Nardi is no stranger to the rules of organized crime.
Not that the Montreal-based actor has portrayed a mob-
ster often, he rarely does, in fact, but because he was born
in Calabria to Old World values. And it's these values of
honour and loyalty that endeared him to one of North
America's most infamous "bosses," Joe Bonanno. In the
film *Bonanno: A Godfather's Story*, the forty-two year old
Nardi portrays the Sicilian Bonanno with glee and convic-
tion, but this insight into the working of the Mafia mentality did not come without some probing. Nardi talks to
us about Joe and son Bill Bonanno, and on how these
"mobsters" are not that much different from any other
immigrant Italian.

*You had the opportunity to meet and speak to Joe
Bonanno.*

Yes, but I was usually in contact with Bill, the son,
because he was the executive producer on the film, so we
had access to him in terms of nuances, what was inherent
in the text. The script was already written for a couple of
years, and of course we always try to get more stuff out
of Bill.

*Did Joe talk about his life, his past, if he felt that what
he did was wrong?*

We didn't get too much into that. Given the context,
it's just so tempting to ask so many questions about so

many things. I was limited to what the script said. I tried to go further at times, but it's a very delicate thing because you want to be able to do the film without carrying a judgment on it, and you always want to get the point of Joe, and the only person who can really shine any light on that is the son, Bill. So a lot of it was trying to get more into the father's headspace.

How is Joe Bonanno these days?

Great. He's ninety-four and he's pretty sharp. He speaks still fluent Italian, and he has incredible conversations with people about freedom and democracy. It's quite astounding.

The series is based on their books where both Joe and Bill admit to their criminal activities. Isn't that risky?

I'm as puzzled as you are on that one. When you read Joe's book, *Man of Honor,* and Bill's book, *Honor Thy Father* by Gay Talese, I think that the way they see it, anyway, that's the way it was explained to me, is that they saw what they did as an infrastructure not unlike the government. They were just working outside the official government, but not that they behaved in any way differently than any governmental institution, any government in any country. They actually see it as something that's as ethical; I don't think there's a perception that what they're doing is morally inferior to the way a government and a head of state operates.

What I find startling is that they admit that Sam Giancana killed John F. Kennedy. That's pretty controversial stuff.

That was one of the more intriguing points of the script. And the other thing, it's very odd because there are so many movies on the mob, and here you have the story, that is so much like *The Godfather*. A lot of information at that time, information about Joe Bonanno, had managed to reach the ears of some of those people who wrote some of those mob movies, including *The Godfather* because there are literally sequences which were used in *The Godfather*. Only this is the real McCoy, and now we're talking about the Kennedy assassination. I read this thing in the *New York Times* last week, which pretty much puts Joe Kennedy in the head of one of the greatest decisions in the history of the century. And his actions proved to be his sons' tragedy.

It seems that since Frank Sinatra died a lot of secrets are being released.

Definitely. It's so funny, because every time I got a chance to speak with Bill and Joe, it was out of a history book. Joe is pretty hard to understand because he's still got a pretty thick accent, but *Showtime* did twenty-five hours of interviews with him and two or three hours of that was given to us as research material. There's something unbelievable about hearing him talk because he's talking about people like Lucky Luciano, American myths on the one hand but real people. And here's a character, Joe Bonanno, who takes you through the entire history.

How hard was it for you not to ask Joe Bonanno sensitive questions about his past?

When it came time to do the film, the hard thing for me was just to have any kind of judgment, because it would probably make for a very weird project. It was very hard because you don't know what to ask and what not to ask, and what's okay to ask. I limited myself to what the script said, how the scene would actually play out in real life, trying to give it a more nuanced reading of the text, the action.

What is your personal opinion of Joe?

One thing is for sure, for those of us who know that kind of generation of older Italians, anybody over seventy, Joe is no different in that when you meet him you get the sense that this man is definitely old world, they use the word "tradition," very clear about his beliefs. Honest to God, when I read the script I expected sort of a character right out of a Martin Scorsese film, instead I was astounded at how Italian he was. That was shocking to me because I usually had the perception that in the States when you left Italy you wanted to assimilate. Instead here's this guy, almost like in Toronto or Montreal, that maintains his Italian, insists that his kids speak Italian, with very Old World values. Another thing that was shocking was how incredibly educated he was for that generation, and most of which I understand was self-taught. Here's a guy that was constantly shocking me about his knowledge of American history, and that didn't fit the image of what I would consider a boss of a family to be like.

Did you like him?

Oh well, he's a fascinating person. He's a very affecting human being. It's bizarre because before I went to his home in Tucson, I saw the way people treated him in interviews, like a Pope, the respect that I saw came with his position. But actually when you see him it's not that kind of blind respect. People actually have a respect for this guy's mind. This guy is sharp, he's got wisdom out of his pores. This is what my grandfather would've been like if he had education. He didn't fit the image of what I had of a character like that.

You visited his hometown of Castellamare in Sicily. Isn't it odd that the heads of so many "families" can come from one small village?

This is what gets interesting with the history of the Sicilian Mafia. But Bill and Joe described that history, on how people from that part of the world in the 1920s managed to have six of the seven heads of families in the States. It's phenomenal. I don't know what it was about Castellamare. Maybe it had a history of brotherhood and resistance to outsiders who tried to take over their territory. It just showed me that, yes, there are things that the mob does, but when you get the perspective from Castellamare you see something that is so ancient, a way of being that is as normal as water. But when that person comes to the States he carries the tradition with him and manages to institute it not only into a hierarchy but also a structure in order to help each other out and make sure that they survive.

Joe must have some amazing stories to tell.

There's this incredible story that he told me. When Joe Kennedy used to smuggle liquor off the coast of Florida, he would throw a boat full of refugees in the water to divert the authorities who would rush to save these people. This gave Kennedy time to bring his stock to land. Joe Bonanno was aghast at this and hated Kennedy every since. Anyway, when Joe came to the States he traveled with this kid. Before leaving Sicily Joe promised this kid's father that he would look after the boy. In

Florida, after they were thrown in the water by Kennedy, Joe and this kid get arrested but up until this kid died a couple of years, they remained friends. His name was Magadino, a cousin to Steven Magadino, the head of the Buffalo family. Until the day of his death, Joe, true to his promise, always made sure that the guy was looked after. It's almost out of folk tales.

That explains the bad karma surrounding Joe Kennedy's family.

What's funny is that the Bonanno family always thought here they were, two families that pretty well started in the same way, made money in the same way, but ended up in different direction. And Joe at the time he meets Joe Kennedy didn't have much respect for him. He actually thought that this guy wasn't ethical at all and that his ways were a lot more honourable.

You're from Calabria. How familiar are you with the Mafia?

There's a huge difference between the Sicilian and the Calabrian Mafia. I think the Sicilian mob has a spirituality attached to it. But it's hard to convince them, the Bonannos, that what they were doing was morally criminal. Take gambling: gambling now is legal. Taking numbers: well lotteries do that now. Alcohol: it's legal. Bill pointed that every activity the mob had in the 1920s, the government sooner or later made legal and took over, and making a killing on them. And they were doing it on their own, protecting their interest in a business venture.

Even the killings?

If you get into how they decide to execute or get rid of someone, they get into how the government gets rid of its own people, how wars are started, how lives are carelessly sacrificed during some insignificant battle somewhere. When they eliminate someone, there's an incredible process that takes place and it's never an easy decision to come by. It's very much like a court of law, people's voices are heard and a vote is taken. Joe was asked by Mike Wallace on *60 Minutes,* what happens when someone from the family has an extramarital affair, and he said in a very sottovoce, "Death." When you talk to him it all seems very legit. I never got the impression talking with Bill that I'm talking to people that have done stuff like that. Obviously they've got muscle, but it was never the muscle talking.

It seems as if you're justifying their methods.

In many ways the code is not unlike the code we have in all Italian families. It's a way of being where there are certain duties and responsibilities that come with being in an Italian family. Now things are changing a little, but there are a lot of people who still live in that world. It's automatic that Sunday you go to your parents, it's automatic that the grandparents watch the kids when the parents go shopping, and when someone dies who's related to someone who's related to someone, you go to the funeral home. Why? It's respect. In many ways it's not that much different from the Bonannos. I expected it to be something so bizarre and different that if my father were to sit down with this man, he would say I can't stay at the table with this man, instead it'll be quite the opposite. I think most of their mentality would be similar.

What does Joe's wife think about her sons following in the father's footsteps?

She adapts. The story that I heard once about the mother, Fanny, is fascinating. Bill had decided to be part of the "family," and because he did and because the younger brother Joe was kinda sucked into it and not as much out of a choice, and because the mother felt that young Joe wasn't really responsible for being part of that "family," when they were in prison, the mother would bring food to Joe but not to Bill. She felt that Bill had made the decision to get into it, and that was her moral standpoint. She felt partly sorry for Joe and felt he needed protection and he got caught up in the whirlwind. And there's no resentment on Bill's part. It's understood.

As an actor you must be weary of doing mob roles.

The three Ms I call it. There's this documentary from RAI Italy that I saw in New York last year called *The Three Ms: Mafia, Mother and Macaroni*, and that most American films are centred around those three themes. Pretty depressing. But I had concerns about doing this. My thing is if the character is defined by something other than his ethnicity, I'll do it. I'll give you an example. There's a series in Quebec called *Omertà* that has 3 million people per episode watching. I turned it down three times because every time I read it I felt that the French-Canadian characters were very well-delineated but the Italian characters were left to do the scenes that had to do with the most stupid cliché vision of what French Canadians thought Italians were. They were written as wops and I'm not interested. When I read the Joe Bonanno story, I felt that there was something that I recognized so much. I recognized the mentality of the man to be not that dissimilar to that of my father or the father of any other

Italian I know of that age. He's an Italian, but the story isn't making fun or celebrating his Italianess. I saw the potential of the story. Here's this guy, ninety-four, well-educated, I didn't know that this kind of beast existed in the States.

Published in Tandem Magazine, *August 1999.*

FILMOGRAHY

Born in 1958, in Calabria, Italy.

- *Almost America* (2001)
- *Bad Faith* (2000)
- *My Father's Angel* (1999)
- *Bonanno: A Godfather's Story* (1999)
- *Angel in a Cage* (1999)
- *La Déroute* (1998)
- *La Bruttina stagionata* (1996)
- *Undertaker* (1996)
- *La Sarrasine* (1992)
- *The Adjuster* (1991)
- *Une histoire inventée* (1990)
- *Cruising Bar* (1989)
- *Brown Bread Sandwiches* (1989)
- *Speaking Parts* (1989)
- *Kalamazoo* (1988)
- *Concrete Angels* (1987)
- *Caffè Italia, Montréal* (1985)
- *Deux super-dingues* (1982)
- *Gas* (1981)

VINCENZO NATALI

Cube

One of the strangest Canadian movies of recent time is a Kafkaesque drama which swerves in and out of dangerous and puzzling situations and which challenges only David Cronenberg in bloody gore. *Cube*, in fact, focuses on six characters who wake up one morning to find themselves thrown into a strange maze made up of identical, symmetrical cube-like rooms. As they try to find the solution to their dilemma, they confront one another and become conflicted by personal turmoil.

"It was an idea I had about five years ago," says *Cube* director/writer Vincenzo Natali. "It came out of the need to make a low-budget film, or what I thought would be a low-budget film. I thought that the kind of movie I wanted to make really lent itself to small budget so then it occurred to me that I could do something, sort of an adventure story or suspense story and set it in one room, or arranging it so one room can substitute for many. That intrigued me but it took a long time to invent a story that would go along with that concept. So it really came out of a pragmatic need."

A graduate of the Canadian Film Centre's 1996 Resident Program, Natali wrote *Cube* with fellow Film Centre graduate Graeme Manson and childhood friend Andre Bijelic. After careful crafting and devising an almost mathematically anal formula, the filmmakers put together a complicated but astute storyline featuring some intensely disturbing characters. In this 14-cubic-foot room there are chambers which lead to more of the same, most of which have lethal built-in traps forcing the "prisoners" to calculate every step they take. Their goal? To find the way out before they run out food, air, water and patience.

"We're never introduced to these people," explains Natali. "They wake up in this bizarre place and they have little memory of who they were before that moment. So slowly their particular skills and memories come to the surface which becomes crucial for their survival."

Featured in this cast of respectable Canucks is David Hewlitt (*Where the Heart Is, The Boys of St. Vincent*) who plays Worth, perhaps the only character with inside knowledge about the Cube; Andrew Miller (*Trial by Jury, Trapped in Paradise*) who portrays the mentally challenged Kazan; Maurice Dean Wint (*Curtis's Charm, Rude*), as the violent Quentin; Nicky Guadagni (*Crash, House*) who plays medical doctor Holloway; and Wayne Robson (*Two If By Sea, Dolores Claiborne*) who's terrific as the methodical Rennes.

"These are difficult roles to master," says Natali. "There isn't much movement here, so the actors have to rely completely on facial and verbal interaction to express their fears and emotions. I was lucky to get these people. They worked so hard in fairly difficult situations."

Also in the cast is young Nicole deBoer (*Brain Candy*) and veteran thesp Julian Richings whose appearance is as brief as his character's death is bloody and memorable.

So the question remains: What's with the cube?

"It's a bit of a mystery," laughs Natali. "It's explored

in the story and indeed we do find out that one of the characters who's in there was involved in the making of it, but even he doesn't have full knowledge of what it is. It's actually never fully revealed. It's always left as a bit of a mystery. For myself and the people I wrote it with, it was more interesting to leave it to create ambiguity so there's room for interpretation."

At the suggestion that the concept lends itself well to stage, Natali bursts out laughing.

"We're working on the *Cube* musical right now," he jokes. "*CUBE!* Except it's sort of an action film too. It's really a weird hybrid. It's weird. It's like this big little movie."

The fifth movie to be developed by the Feature Film Project (*Blood & Donuts, Rude, House, Shoemaker*), *Cube* got most of its financing through the program. So how did Natali get to be the lucky one?

"I keep asking myself that question," he laughs. "It's exactly that. I got incredibly lucky. I happened to be at the right place at the right time. They were very much in need of making a project by the end of the year and I think they liked the short film that I did at the centre two years ago, *Elevated,* which coincidentally took place in a very confined space. I think that showed them that technically and artistically I could pull it off because it's a challenging movie considering that it's so confined."

A Toronto native who dropped out of film school at Ryerson University, Natali quickly established himself as an accomplished storyboard artist which eventually led to a full-time job at famed animation house Nelvana.

"Nelvana was almost like film school for me," says

Natali. "They were very generous there and I learned a tremendous amount just about narrative storytelling. That was a really good experience. I also made enough money to finance my own short films."

Both *Mouth* (1992) and *Playground* (1993) traveled extensively to film festivals around the world, and the recognition the young director acquired allowed him access into the Film Centre.

"It was without a doubt one of the best experiences of my whole life," says Natali. "I'm rather cynical about film school. I went into the Centre with a degree of doubt and cynicism and it turned out to be this incredible experience."

As to his next film . . .

"It's called *Mutants*," he laughs. "Sort of a love story about a geneticist who falls in love with his hybrid creation. I know it sounds silly but it's not supposed to be."

Published in Tandem Magazine, *October 1997.*

FILMOGRAPHY

Born in 1969, in Toronto, Ontario.

- *Cypher* (2002)
- *Nothing* (2002)
- *Bottomfeeders* (2001)
- *Elevated* (1997)
- *Cube* (1997)

CATHERINE O'HARA

Waiting for Guffman

Notable as the self-centered entertainer Lola Heatherton on *SCTV* who always told her audience: "I want to bear your children!", comedienne Catherine O'Hara has been blessed with superb comic timing and a flair for spontaneity. Never have these qualities been put to greater test than her role in *Waiting for Guffman*, Christopher Guest's outrageous satirical comedy.

Shot in twenty-nine days in a small Texan town with one super-16 camera and no script, the film demanded some severely "adventurous" performers. No question O'Hara fit the bill.

"I knew really nothing about the movie except that it had something to do with community theatre," remembers O'Hara about her first meeting with the filmmakers. "Then I met with Chris and Eugene (Levy, co-writer) and they're telling me their story outlines, and I'm going 'Please, can I be in this? Please!' Hearing about it was too much fun to be left out."

What else can one expect from Guest, one of the creative forces behind the comedy mockumentary *This Is Spinal Tap,* and a one-time cast member of *Saturday Night Live?* For *Waiting for Guffman,* Guest and Levy assembled eight actors in Lockhart, Texas, with an outline of characters and some key plot points, pointed the camera and just rolled. The result is one of the most side-split-ting comedies of the decade.

In essence, the movie follows the antics of failed stage director Corky St. Clair (Guest) who stages a musical review commemorating 150 years of his town's history under the watchful eye of a documentary crew covering the sesquicentennial events.

"He's amazingly restrained because I know how funny he is," says O'Hara of Guest. "His brain doesn't stop coming up with incredible, funny stuff."

O'Hara plays Sheila Albertson, married to fellow travel agent, Ron (Fred Willard), both who audition for the musical with a duet version of "Midnight at the Oasis."

"It's so sad when you're good at being bad," laughs O'Hara. "We had to actually rehearse these auditions; Chris and Eugene didn't see them beforehand. So me and Fred are actually trying to get laughs for being bad, but at the same time we had to do our choreography. Fred was so serious, he wanted to wear the towels around his neck and I was so nervous."

Also starring Parker Posey, Matt Keesler, Bob Balaban and Lewis Arquette, *Waiting for Guffman* is astoundingly coherent for a pic that had next-to-no concept.

"That's because Chris has amazing faith in the people he hires," says O'Hara. "He didn't force anything on anyone letting people just flow with whatever came out. Nothing was planned. Chris shot a lot of stuff really wide because he didn't know what anyone was going to do, including himself. He's used to catching spontaneous stuff, that's why he kept shooting wide. He just kept hanging on to stuff that was happening. Just the pure freedom of it, excellent self-indulgent fun."

Born into a family of artistic talents (brother Marcus was a documentary director and sister Mary Margaret is an internationally renowned pop singer), O'Hara came into showbiz the old-fashioned way: via waitressing. While cleaning tables at Second City theatre in Toronto, O'Hara managed to convince troupe member John Candy to listen to her routines eventually joining the cast in 1973. In 1976, she was a member of the highly successful TV series, *SCTV*, until 1983, creating such memorable characters as Lola Heatherton, Maureen Wallace the *SCTV* P.R. person, Lorna Minelli and Dusty Towne.

"By the time I left the show I was ready to do something else," remembers the Toronto native. "I was dying to do something longer than five or eight minutes, and wanting to get deeper into a character."

Before *Waiting for Guffman*, O'Hara has been cast in cinematic roles that really haven't drawn on her abilities. She was a hysterically vengeful barmaid in *After Hours*; an activist yuppie in *Beetlejuice* (on the set of which she met husband Bo Welch, Tim Burton's art director); a grotesque distaff criminal in *Dick Tracy*; and Calamity Jane in *Tall Tale*. But her most prosperous role to date may be as Macaulay Culkin's mom in the *Home Alone* movies.

"What can I say?" smiles O'Hara. "My roles were really small. They wanted Macaulay to be with the crooks, that's really what they wanted. They just needed to use the parents to get them there. I know they wrote a third sequel, *It's Crazy*. We've lost him too many times, otherwise I'd be going to prison for losing him so often."

So there's little question that *Waiting for Guffman*, a true vehicle for her terrific mimic abilities, is O'Hara's dream project?

"Oh God, yes," she smiles. "It would be like a gift from heaven to be able to do one of these a year."

Published in Access Magazine, *February 1997.*

FILMOGRAPHY

Born March 4, 1954, in Toronto, Ontario.

- *A Mighty Wind* (2003)
- *Searching for Debra Winger* (2002)
- *Orange County* (2001)
- *Speaking of Sex* (2001)
- *Edwurd Fudwupper Fibbed Big* (2000)
- *Best in Show* (2000)
- *Bartok the Magnificent* (1999)
- *The Life Before This* (1999)
- *Home Fries* (1998)
- *Pippi Longstocking* (1997)
- *The Last of the High Kings* (1996)
- *Waiting for Guffman* (1996)
- *Tall Tale* (1995)
- *A Simple Twist of Fate* (1994)
- *Wyatt Earp* (1994)
- *The Paper* (1994)
- *The Nightmare Before Christmas* (1993)
- *There Goes the Neighborhood* (1992)
- *Home Alone 2: Lost in New York* (1992)
- *Betsy's Wedding* (1990)
- *Little Vegas* (1990)
- *Home Alone* (1990)
- *Dick Tracy* (1990)
- *Beetlejuice* (1988)

- *Heartburn* (1986)
- *After Hours* (1985)
- *Double Negative* (1980)
- *Nothing Personal* (1980)

Marina Orsini

Dr. Lucille: The Lucille Teasdale Story

Marina Orsini portrays Canada's indefatigable Lucille Teasdale.

The Human Rights Commission lists her next to Mother Theresa as one of the world's most humanitarian women; while Italy has bestowed upon her, a non-Italian, one of that country's most coveted honours, the Ordine al Merito.

So how is that many of us have never heard of Lucille Teasdale?

"It's always quite shocking to find out that people like her, a person with that kind of life, we've never heard of," says Italian-Canadian actress Marina Orsini, who portrays Teasdale in *Dr. Lucille: The Lucille Teasdale Story*. "And it's about time we talk about people like her. I'm sure that out there in the world there are other Lucilles and other Pieros [Piero Corti was Lucille's Italian husband]. Unfortunately we don't hear about them until very late."

And such is the case with Teasdale. Born in Montreal in 1929, the fourth of seven children, Lucille was the unwanted daughter of a severely depressed mother. She escaped her hostile household by hanging out with nuns who had recently returned from missionary work in China. This was to inspire the young girl's life forever.

In Canada of the 1950s medicine was a man's profession, but this didn't stop Lucille from studying pediatric surgery. It was as an intern at Montreal's Sainte-Justine Hospital that she met the handsome Piero Corti, a doctor from Italy looking for a surgeon to work with him in a small African bush clinic he was hoping to transform into a hospital for the poor.

Unable to find a position in Canada or the U.S., Lucille took a job in the south of France and, infatuated with Piero, arranged to meet with him in Marseilles. This time Piero asked the young Canadian to join him for a two-month mission in Uganda. She accepted, and remained for the rest of her life.

The couple had an enormous task ahead of them. Side-by-side they administered to the poor and suffering, and managed to survive the reign of terror of Idi Amin Dada's dictatorship. And as their tiny hospital grew, thanks to donations from Italy and Canada, Lucille and Piero fell in love, got married and had a daughter, Dominique, who today works as a doctor in Italy.

In the 1980s the political situation in Uganda worsened under Dada's successor, Milton Obote, and both Piero and Lucille fought tirelessly to save the wounded of the ensuing civil war. AIDS was still undiscovered, and Lucille continued to perform surgeries unaware that the cuts she endured were to become lethal. She was diagnosed with the AIDS virus in 1985 but continued to perform surgeries and raise money for St-Mary's-Lacor hospital until her death in 1996.

Before succumbing to the illness, Lucille and Piero also received from Italy the humanitarian award by Accademia Nazionale dei Lincei for "exceptional undertaking and high moral and humanitarian value." Lucille also received the Order of Canada and the Order of Quebec.

Today she is buried near her beloved hospital in war-torn Uganda.

"We were unable to visit Saint-Mary's," says Orsini. "We weren't even allowed in the country. Even Piero can't go back there to her grave as often as he wants to."

Dr. Lucille: The Lucille Teasdale Story was filmed almost entirely in South Africa, with Corti himself assisting on the pre-production. It was during this time that Orsini had a chance to ask the famed humanitarian questions about his remarkable wife.

"He's a fabulous man, a very generous human being," says Orsini. "He was very happy to share with me and Massimo (Ghini, who portrays Corti in the film) his life in Africa. They were great and unforgettable moments. I was quite privileged to spend that time with him. Everything that they built they wouldn't have been able to have done without each other. They really needed each other. It's thanks to what they had together that they did what they did. She will always be a great part of his life."

And how did portraying Lucille Teasdale affect the life of Orsini, celebrated in her native Quebec as one of that province's most acclaimed actresses (*Le Filles de Caleb, Black Harbour, The Sleep Room, Shehaweh*)?

"You know, when they approached me for the film I was touched. I fell in love with the woman. When I was offered the role I cried," admits Marina. "Playing her I really got a chance to taste and to feel what was her source of inspiration and what was her goal, her challenges. Being a woman in the 1950s, going into medicine, wanting to be a surgeon was quite something. It was almost unheard of. Not many women were able to go through all the difficulties. What amazes me always is the strength, the determination, the courage of the life that she and Piero had. And the choices they made. They really chose that life. Their immense humanity is something that I was really even more amazed of."

But, Orsini proudly offers, she has something in common with Lucille, and that is her background. In fact like Lucille and Piero, Marina's mother is French Canadian and her dad was Italian. "My dad came to Canada from San Martino near Ascoli Piceno when he was sixteen right after the war," says Orsini. "He fell in love with my mom, got married, and never went back to Italy. But I fell in love with his side of the family. We'd go to Italy every two years, and I studied Italian on Saturday mornings as kid. I love all my relatives."

So how did her Italian-language skills fare up with her charismatic co-star Ghini (*Tea with Mussolini, Up at the Villa*), today one of Italy's most sought-after stars?

"He was great," she admits. "The minute we met we spoke in Italian. I couldn't resist him. He's so charming. He's a great man, a great partner to work with. That was another treat about doing the film."

Many a fan will agree with her on that.

Published in Tandem Magazine, *April 2000.*

FILMOGRAPHY

Born January 4, 1967, in Ville-Émard, Quebec.

- *Dr. Lucille: The Lucille Teasdale Story* (2000)
- *Les Muses orphelines* (2000)
- *The Sleep Room* (1998)
- *Tous pour un* (1995)
- *Eddie and the Cruisers II: Eddie Lives!* (1989)
- *Grenouille et la baleine* (1987)

JEREMY PODESWA

The Five Senses

When local filmmaker Jeremy Podeswa released *Eclipse*, his first feature, he became an instant phenomenon with lovers of cinema brave and quirky. From the layer-upon-layer tale about a group of people affected by an oncoming eclipse, to the hypnotic cinematography, *Eclipse* became another feather in the proud Canadian filmmaking cap. With his newest film, *The Five Senses*, Podeswa has matured into a more sensitive and subtle filmmaker, but still retaining that edge for narrative and atmospheric moviemaking.

The Five Senses, which opened the Perspective Canada programme at this year's Toronto International Film Festival, deals with the five senses, touch, taste, hearing, smell, vision, as analyzed through the lives of various, but connected, individuals.

Where did the idea for The Five Senses *come from?*

I liked the idea about doing something around the senses. There's something very evocative and something that's immediately poetic and metaphorical about them. I also like the narrative possibilities about having five characters each representing the various different senses and thinking on how that could play out dramatically. There are the obvious things, like somebody who has a heightened sense of something, or somebody who's losing a sense. That's very dramatic, of course. But there are many subtle things you can do as well. I created this massage therapist (played by Gabrielle Rose) whose whole being is based on touching people and yet she isn't able to be touched herself and isn't able to touch somebody intimately for a long time. And she also has a daughter (Nadia Litz) who she can't touch physically or emotionally in any way. So the irony of her story being completely about touch and about her being completely separated from that, is something that is very appealing to me dramatically.

In the film, as in Eclipse, *you deal with issues of fear and anxiety. Why the concern?*

It's part of this contemporary anxiety that everybody has these days. These are dangerous times, the newspapers are full of horrible things, and in the movie we have the story of a missing child. That's a really profound urban anxiety. A lot of single women have fears of never finding a man, and single men have fears of never finding a mate. There are all kinds of anxieties we have; do we have a good job, do we make enough money, living our life to the fullest? We have more advantages than any other generation in our society, and yet we have much more anxiety, there's more pressure. What I'm doing really is reflecting the popular culture, so it's certainly part of my life and a lot of people that I know. But at the same time I don't only what to raise that stuff up and make something that's negative. In fact, I show that there is a way out, and that's getting back to basics.

What sparked the idea for you make The Five Senses?

Two events. One is a trip I took with my producer Camelia Frieberg, down the coast of California where she had arranged to meet a woman she hadn't seen in twenty years. Through this woman she ends up meeting the guy who would become her husband, and I was there when they met. Through that whole encounter, witnessing what seems a match made in heaven brought together by this very convoluted series of circumstances, I really started to think a lot about destiny and fate and why people come together. I'm very into the idea that everything that you do has consequences in your life. It may not be apparent then, but it becomes apparent much later. All that stuff, plus the general rules of destiny, love and fate did it for me.

And the other event?

My travels when I went on this big festival road trip for *Eclipse* for a year and half. I was travelling a lot on my own and during that period I was cut off from my family and friends and other kinds of work I would normally do, living this strange kind of life. I was in almost complete isolation going to all these new places all the time, meeting a whack of new people and having these very intense and very superficial relationships. While I was there I interrogated my own idea of what do relationships really mean, what are the things that really matter to you in the world generally. I had a lot of time to think about that stuff, and because I was separated from all my normal relationships I had an objective view of what they were really like. I was thinking about what my values are specifically in regards to people in my life. Who means something to me and who doesn't, and who did I miss while I was travelling and who didn't I miss? My romantic life was shot to hell while I was travelling, so I was starting to think about what that meant and where I was prioritizing that in regards to my life.

As with Eclipse, *this time you again use overlapping narratives. Why?*

I always liked these multi-character stories where you deal with big issues because then you can tackle a really big subject and you can have four or five or six fractured viewpoints on the subject. If you had just one main protagonist, you would have only one point of view on, say, love. I like the idea about saying something about love, but having a prismatic view on that so you have four or five or six characters grappling about love and then it's interesting for the audience because everybody's got a point of entry into the movie, but it's not always the same. It's interesting for me to make it all encompassing and show that these subjects are hugely universal.

One of the stories is that of a woman, played by Mary Louise Parker, who makes tasteless cakes and who gets involved with an enthusiastic Italian, Marco Leonardi.

So much of relationships is about projection, and she's a character who always had commitment issues and can't believe that people are really in love with her. She obviously doesn't trust men and doesn't trust her own feelings, she's coming into this relationship with a lot of baggage, and he's here without any baggage at all. But she's completely suspicious. That's her problem, and the interesting thing is to see if she conquers this problem. There's a lot of pathos in that.

I love the story about the optometrist, played by Philippe Volger, who's going deaf, but who finds hope in the end.

Much of how we experience life is what we bring to it. So much is about perception and if you perceive that you won't have any more enjoyment out of life, then you won't. But if you don't perceive it that way you can go on to have a very full and fabulous life. And that's what happens to him.

Published in Tandem Magazine, *September 1999.*

FILMOGRAPHY

Born in 1962, in Toronto, Ontario.

- *The Susan Smith Tapes* (2001)
- *Touch* (2001)
- *24fps* (2000)
- *The Five Senses* (1999)
- *Eclipse* (1994)
- *Caveman Rainbow* (1993)
- *Walls* (1993)
- *Standards* (1992)
- *Diamond Time* (1985)
- *In the Name of Bobby* (1985)
- *The Revelations of Becka Paulsen* (1985)
- *Nion* (1984)
- *David Roche Talks to You About Love* (1983)

SARAH POLLEY

The Sweet Hereafter

Don't ever refer to her as the "little ingenue" as they did at the Cannes Film Festival where she promoted her latest film, Atom Egoyan's *The Sweet Hereafter*; and definitely don't remind her of Sara Stanley, the character she portrayed on *Road to Avonlea* for so many years.

Sarah Polley, at the still tender age of nineteen, is anything but the syrupy sweet thing most Canadian television viewers would like to believe she is. A political activist who's been fighting head-first against the right-wing forces of the Toronto government since she was an adolescent, Polley has also made it a point recently of selecting film roles that are as far removed from the *Green Gables* world as flies are from fire.

"I'm tired of having to compare every single thing I do to Avonlea," says an exasperated Polley from her home in Toronto. "I think that I'll have to live with that my whole life. Every single thing I do will be the '*Road from Avonlea*,' or 'We're not in Avonlea anymore.' In terms of my own consciousness, I've been out of Avonlea since before I even did it. I was never in Avonlea personally."

Since quitting the long-running television series, Polley has portrayed racier and meatier characters on Egoyan's *Exotica* and Peter Wellington's *Joe's So Mean to Josephine*. But her most controversial role to date is arguably that of Nicole Burnell from *The Sweet Hereafter*.

Based on the book by Russell Banks, and inspired from a true story, the film focuses on a big-city lawyer (Ian Holm) who provokes a rural community into suing authorities after a school bus crash kills fourteen children. One of the survivors, Nicole, is left half-paralyzed tragically adding to the fact that she's been having an ongoing incestuous relationship with her father (Tom McCamus).

"I wasn't worried about the character itself," explains Polley about any misgivings she might have had in portraying Nicole. "But looking at the piece as a whole, looking at the script, looking at the cast and looking at Adam's work and seeing what a huge talent it was to rise to that standard of crafting a film. From what I read through the script, and from the cast, and him, I couldn't see any flaws in the movie itself. I thought it was going to be a fantastic movie from the outset, and I was nervous being the part of it that would screw it up."

Which she certainly didn't do considering *The Sweet Hereafter* walked away with the Grand Prix at Cannes, the Festival's second-most prestigious award, and the first time ever for a Canadian film.

"I also like the fact that there were no sexually graphic scenes in the movie considering the subject matter," continues Polley. "There is one scene where my father and I are kissing but it's very tastefully done. That scene is needed to establish the relationship. What is disturbing about the scene to most people is the fact that it's very romantic, and I think people have the freedom to misinterpret that. For me, watching it, makes the incest that much more disturbing."

But the hardest aspect of the role wasn't the character she was to portray, stresses Polley. It was the realization that maybe, for the first time, she was being asked to act.

"This is the first time I treated acting as a craft," she admits. "I think when you're younger, you have a sense of being able to portray yourself. This was the first time I had to prepare myself to creating a character, and to be aware of the technical aspects of what it is to be in front of a camera. That was made more important to me by watching somebody like Ian Holm who really is an artist. He really has a very intense grasp on the craft and I was forced to watch that and maybe realize that I haven't been taking it seriously enough and that it can be something quite great."

An unusual comment from someone who's grown up in a family of actors. Polley remembers, in fact, learning to read from playing with her mother's scripts. (Diane Polley died of cancer three years ago.)

"My whole way of learning was to put it through dialogue because I had a really good memory for it," remembers Polley. "From an early age the idea of a script and acting was imprinted on me. But my parents really didn't want me to get involved in acting and ended up relenting when it was evident that I was going to do it. I was five when they gave in and I've been begging to do it since I was three."

Her debut came in the movie *One Magic Christmas* and continued with *Big Town, Babar: The Movie, The Adventures of Baron Munchausen, Lantern Hill* and the television series *Ramona* and *Road to Avonlea*. A couple of years ago Sarah took a break from acting to get treatment for a back ailment that has plagued her for many years, scoliosis.

"I had to have major surgery a couple of years ago. It was the most painful thing I had to go through," she says. "Before the operation I was pretty slumped over on one side, you couldn't help notice it. It was awful."

Having lived on her own since the age fourteen, lost her mother at ten, and having worked as a professional actor since the age five, Polley admits that her life hasn't been particularly easy.

"There are some things that I wouldn't let my kids do from my own experience," she says. "I don't think I'd let them act. It's a very weird way to grow up. It's a disturbing mixture of being really used and at the same time really pampered so it's being treated really badly and really overly well at the same time. I don't think either thing is very healthy when you're growing up. It's a very false world to live in. People tend to become very isolated from the rest of the world, and people in show business tend to not be able to see very far outside of it. I'm still grappling with that myself and trying to expose myself to as many things other than acting as possible."

One of which is political activism. Since the age fifteen Polley has been a fervent supporter of the New Democratic Party by spending time at Kensington Market selling copies of *The Socialist Worker* and hanging around Queen's Park protesting cuts in social services and education. One of her few regrets is that she wasn't able to do as much campaigning during this past summer's elections because of her commitments at Cannes.

"I feel that Mike Harris being elected is reason enough for anybody to be active," she laughs. "There are points where I put political activism definitely above acting. I've always been pretty conscious of issues like that, just from my family. I couldn't let things happen without raising my voice even if nobody hears it. I just rather know that I was doing something even if it wasn't going to make a difference."

Published in Menz Magazine, *September 1997.*

FILMOGRAPHY

Born on January 8, 1979, in Toronto, Ontario.

- *The I Inside* (2003)
- *The Event* (2002)
- *Luck* (2002)
- *My Life Without Me* (2002)
- *No Such Thing* (2001)
- *This Might Be Good* (2000)
- *The Claim* (2000)
- *The Law of Enclosures* (2000)
- *Love Come Down* (2000)
- *The Weight of Water* (2000)
- *The Life Before This* (1999)
- *Guinevere* (1999)
- *Go* (1999)
- *eXistenZ* (1999)
- *Last Night* (1998)
- *Jerry and Tom* (1998)
- *The Planet of Junior Brown* (1997)
- *The Hanging Garden* (1997)

- *The Sweet Hereafter* (1997)
- *Joe's So Mean to Josephine* (1996)
- *Exotica* (1994)
- *The Adventures of Baron Munchausen* (1988)
- *The Big Town* (1987)
- *Blue Monkey* (1987)
- *Heaven on Earth* (1987)
- *Prettykill* (1987)
- *One Magic Christmas* (1985)

KEANU REEVES

The Gift

Toronto's own Keanu Reeves is certainly one of Hollywood's most puzzling cats. Although there's little question he's a cutie, most people tend to forget that he's also a damned good actor. Forget *Bill & Ted's Excellent Adventure*, funny material is not always easy to act out, and Reeves has acted in some terrific and difficult films, including Tim Hunter's *River's Edge* and Gus Van Sant's *My Own Private Idaho*.

"My reputation as being 'stupid' is a direct result of certain interviews," admits the thirty-seven year old actor. "But reality is I just get bored with them. Sure, my answers tend to be monosyllabic, but that's because most of the questions are really dumb."

No argument there. So this scribe is going to try and mentally stimulate the man as best she can. This isn't such a hard task, considering the pic we're talking about features one of Reeves' most unusual performances. In Sam Raimi's *The Gift*, in fact, we see a Keanu that is evil and violent as he portrays wife-beating redneck Donnie Barksdale. Not a product of a violent family himself, it's interesting to find out where Reeves found the inspiration for his character.

"I did look at what it would be like if I was abused and maybe what that would create in an adult," he explains about his research. "I went to Savannah three weeks early and tried to find out, search for Donnie Barksdale. I arranged to meet with this couple that dealt with spousal abuse because I wanted to find out clinically what are some of the defining things that you would find in the male and in the female in spousal abuse. Then I got in the truck, changed my clothes and started to hang. As well as trying to find Donnie Barksdale, I was trying to find an authenticity to a character and a vocality. I found this one particular county called Rankin and that's where I ended up finding the 'real' Donnie Barksdale."

In *The Gift*, Donnie is the catalyst behind Annie Wilson's (Cate Blanchett) problems. Annie is a psychic in this small Georgia town, and one of her most regular customers is Donnie's wife (played by Hilary Swank) who sees in Annie an escape route from her violent spouse. In order to keep his wife in check, Donnie must first keep Annie away, even that means threatening violence and death.

"Physical violence is not something that I practice all the time so that, for me, was hard," jokes Reeves. "But the way that we did it was just me and Hilary Swank and Raimi in a room in a trailer, starting with an improvisation. He said, 'Let's have a scene with the Barksdales at home,' and in that event it was, 'Did you go see that woman?' 'No.' 'Liar.' 'Donnie, we just had a talk. We didn't talk about us.' 'Liar.' Then Raimi would say: 'Every time you say 'liar' you're negotiating with her. Don't be polite. Just hit her.' So I did. 'Liar.' Pop, pop. It's very complicated. I do know that power is intoxicating and that the physical power that a man can have sometimes over a woman can be scary. To get in touch with that and see that, there's always that line. Every person has all the characters within themselves, the human traits within themselves whether it's been quiet or in the forefront, but the potential is there. That's scary."

What's also scary is a scene in *The Gift* where Donnie punches Annie in the stomach with such a force to cause gasps of horror in the audience.

"That was really hard for me to do," admits Reeves. "The sequences where I was beating up Hilary were easier, there were safety devices when I pulled her up by the hair, there was a handle that I could grab inside her wig, so I was able to play in the expression of violence. When I had to walk up to Cate, I had to punch her, a stage punch but still, I had to hit a woman ostensibly in the womb and that, psychologically, was just a hard barrier to cross. But we got the shot. That's one of the great things about Cate. She said, 'Let's go there, let's do this,' to make that okay."

Born in Beirut by showgirl mom, Patricia, Reeves didn't have much of a relationship with his dad (Samuel Reeves is currently serving a jail sentence for cocaine possession). After his little sister, Kim, was born, Reeves moved with his mom to New York City where Patricia met and married director Paul Aaron. Eventually the entire family would move to Toronto where Keanu would attend (but not complete) Jarvis Collegiate high school. (Patricia has since divorced and married at least twice.)

Unable to get a job with the Second City Touring Company, Reeves turned his attention to Toronto's independent stage landing his first role in Theatre Passe Muraille's production of *Wolfboy,* featuring homo-erotic undertones. The incentive to move to Los Angeles came after Reeves landed a small part in the hockey feature *Youngblood*, starring Rob Lowe.

Keanu quickly landed lead roles in indie films such as *Permanent Record* and *The Prince of Pennsylvania*, soon rising to more prominent features such as *Dangerous Liaisons, Parenthood* and *I Love You To Death.* The rest (*Point Break, Speed, The Matrix*, etc.) is pure box-office success.

As to his personal life, "Let's not go there," says Reeves. "So far this interview's been good. Is it that important who I date and how I pass my days? I find that attention for my personal life rises when a film comes out and leaves when the film is over. I always find it weird when a stranger asks me personal questions. I don't mind speaking about work, but not personal."

Fair enough. But I gotta ask, "Are you dating?"

"Yeah," he smiles. "A French actress. Her name is Amanda De Cadenet." Now that wasn't so hard, was it?

Published in Tandem Magazine, *January, 2001.*

FILMOGRAPHY

Born on September 2, 1964, in Beirut, Lebanon.

- *The Matrix Revolutions* (2003)
- *Mayor of Sunset Strip* (2003)
- *Matrix Reloaded* (2003)
- *Hardball* (2001)
- *Sweet November* (2001)
- *The Gift* (2000)

- *The Watcher* (2000)
- *The Replacements* (2002)
- *The Matrix* (1999)
- *Me and Will* (1998)
- *The Devil's Advocate* (1997)
- *The Last Time I Committed Suicide* (1997)
- *Feeling Minnesota* (1996)
- *Chain Reaction* (1996)
- *A Walk in the Clouds* (1995)
- *Johnny Mnemonic* (1995)
- *Speed* (1994)
- *Little Buddha* (1993)
- *Even Cowgirls Get the Blues* (1993)
- *Freaked* (1993)
- *Much Ado About Nothing* (1993)
- *Dracula* (1992)
- *Providence* (1991)
- *My Own Private Idaho* (1991)
- *Bill & Ted's Excellent Journey* (1991)
- *Point Break* (1991)
- *Tune in Tomorrow* (1990)
- *I Love You to Death* (1990)
- *Parenthood* (1989)
- *Bill & Ted's Excellent Adventure* (1989)
- *The Night Before* (1988)
- *Permanent Record* (1988)
- *The Prince of Pennsylvania* (1988)
- *Dangerous Liaisons* (1988)
- *Flying* (1986)
- *River's Edge* (1986)
- *Youngblood* (1986)
- *One Step Away* (1985)

BRUNO RUBEO

Pushing Tin

Toronto has churned out many Hollywood success stories (Jim Cameron and Jim Carrey come easily to mind), some of which only few people are aware of. Take Bruno Rubeo, for example. An Academy Award-nominated production designer (for *Driving Miss Daisy*), Rubeo is one of tinsel town's most sought-after designers having bestowed his artistry to such high-budget movies as *The Devil's Advocate*, *Dolores Clairborne*, *The Client*, *Sommersby* and *Kindergarten Cop*.

How many of us were aware that he sharpened his chops at our very own Channel 47?

"Toronto was an accident," laughs Rubeo from the set of his new movie, *Pushing Tin*, currently shooting in T.O. "I had moved to New York from Rome and I was on my way to Los Angeles. I stopped in Toronto because I wanted to take my time and visit Canada. The first day I arrived in Toronto I phoned Dan Iannuzzi and Elena Caprile who were friends of a cousin of mine from Rome. We got together and they told me they had just started a television station with these multilingual programs and they needed an art director. I started art directing for them immediately, the next day."

Rubeo remained three years with Channel 47 and then did a stint as a freelancer for another six years before deciding it was time to pursue his original goal: a film career in Los Angeles. Born and raised in Rome, Rubeo came to movies by accident. Originally intent on becoming an electronic engineer, he had enrolled at the city's scientific lyceum when he came across a poster posted in the school lobby.

"It was advertising this new experimental government film school called Istituto Statale di Cinematografia," remembers Rubeo. "As a kid I was always interested in science and art and when I saw the poster of the film school I immediately realized that that's what I wanted to do. I think movies combine both, art and science. So I quit the lyceum, enrolled in the film school and from that moment I had no doubt that that was what I wanted to do."

After graduation, Rubeo did work with Carlo Rambaldi on *Conan the Destroyer* and *Dune*, but soon found himself on a flight to New York with his new American bride. There he abandoned his cinematic dreams to pursue a career in advertising which lasted only as long as his marriage. It was at that point that he decided to it was time to head west to Los Angeles and get back into moviemaking, then came that fateful pit-stop in Toronto.

"It's strange being back here," says Rubeo. "I always liked Toronto, but you never know when you're going to be back. Staying for six months feels like I'm living here again, it's like going back in time. That's strange."

But worth it. *Pushing Tin* is the new movie by British director Mike Newell (*Four Weddings and a Funeral*) and which stars John Cusack and Billy Bob Thornton. The true story of air-traffic controllers who rebel against government regulation, the film poses new challenges for Rubeo.

"We had to do a lot of research on air traffic controlling and what it's all about," he says. "We had to study what the radar means and what all those graphics means. We had to go to those places where they did this kind of work and we had to talk to technicians, radar operators, pilots and all kinds of people to find out as much as possible. In the case of *The Devil's Advocate*, for example, there is not that much research aside from artistic research, to decide how the movie should look. As soon as you decide on a style then you go and do research on that style and hopefully you come up with your own idea, your own style."

Which brings us to his big break. After having moved to Los Angeles, Rubeo managed to get work on dozens of minor films, including Joseph Scanlan's *Spring Fever* and Eric Weston's *Moon Goddess*.

"In Los Angeles you can have a ton of experience, but your career doesn't go anywhere if the films don't go anywhere," says Rubeo. "You have to have a lot of luck. Of course talent has a lot to do with it, but you need luck to become associated with a successful movie."

His luck was meeting *Moon Goddess* producer Gerald Green who asked the production designer to work on his next movie by a new director. The film was called *Salvador* and the director was Oliver Stone. Stone was so impressed with Rubeo's work, that he immediately hired him to work on his follow-up political flick, the Academy Award-winning *Platoon*.

"That was it," smiles Rubeo. "That's what really launched my career."

Although Rubeo continued to work for Stone (*Talk

Radio, Born on the Fourth of July), the designer's schedule has since been filling up at a break-neck speed.

"It's come to a point where I have to plan time off," he admits. "What I tell my agent is don't tell me what happens because I'm taking time off. If I've done two back-to-back movies without a break, I want to take two or three months off and go to Italy. So I tell my agent not to even tell me what a potential project is because if it's interesting it would be hard for me to say no."

Published in Tandem Magazine, *March 1998.*

FILMOGRAPHY

Born in Italy.

- *The Great Raid* (2002)
- *Proof of Life* (2000)
- *The Thomas Crown Affair* (1999)
- *Pushing Tin* (1999)
- *The Devil's Advocate* (1997)
- *The Evening Star* (1996)
- *Dolores Claiborne* (1995)
- *The Client* (1994)
- *Bound by Honor* (1993)
- *Sommersby* (1993)
- *Kindergarten Cop* (1990)
- *Born on the Fourth of July* (1989)
- *Driving Miss Daisy* (1989)
- *Old Gringo* (1989)
- *Blood Red* (1988)
- *Talk Radio* (1988)
- *Walker* (1987)
- *Platoon* (1986)
- *Salvador* (1986)
- *Spring Fever* (1982)

STEVE SANGUEDOLCE

Smack

We're both in disbelief. Me in hearing that for filmmaker Steve Sanguedolce butchering your own animals in the basement of your North York home was a normal occurrence when he was a child. Him for hearing that this scribe, of his same generation and also a member of the Italian-Canadian Toronto community, had not only never experienced such a thing, but has never heard of it either.

"I think it was very typical of a lot of Italian Canadians' experiences," says Sanguedolce. "There were animals in the house and we foolishly as children thought they were pets. You see, we had a cousin who was a butcher so he'd come over and slaughter the sheep, rabbits, geese and goats we had in our basement. I know a lot of people who had a lot of animals who slaughtered them regularly. My parents are Sicilian and so they lived on a farm. They had their own animals, they slaughtered their own meat, they had their own milk and made their own cheese. So this was a way of life they exported into Toronto. It has since changed. I don't know how many others continue to slaughter their own animals in their own homes. But I saw a lot of it as a kid. I think it must have affected me in some way because I had a much different relationship to animals than I had then."

I guess ordinary pets like cats and dogs were out of the question for the Sanguedolce household.

"Definitely," laughs the forty year old Steve. "What's really scary is hearing about one kid in school, Italian as well, and he'd talk about having all these cats that would get really fat after a year, like baby pigs. Then they'd miraculously disappear. The luxury of pets is something that doesn't exist in a more peasant, southern culture. I have two little dogs, and my parents don't want me to bring them to their house."

Slaughtering animals is an important element in Sanguedolce's latest experimental effort, *Smack*, the story of three brothers who take different paths in life. "The first character in the film, Antonio, almost seems distinct from the other two," explains Steve. "He's a little straighter, has more of a religious conscience, and he tries to get out of it as it's starting. And a lot of that has to do with the traumatic experiences as a child when he saw so many things that he loved being killed and kind of learned to equate the two in some way."

Antonio, in fact, is the semi-autobiographical creation of Steve's twin brother, Sam Sanguedolce, who provides the narrative to the character.

"We were taught that slaughter was part of life," he says. "We didn't have a concept of pets as kids and those stories that Antonio says, those are our stories from my childhood. It's as if anything that you've become close to and learned to love is killed, and that's a kind of common, acceptable place to be. When love is held adjacent to death then you can almost understand in some way why somebody might move into a more dramatic or drastic existence, doing drugs and being rebellious and destructive. Those are the only things that I think are really important to children in terms of bonding, closeness, innocence. And when it's taken away at that level you can see how that can be construed in that destructive way."

Smack is an unconventional movie detailing the lives of Antonio, Sybil (Paul Dileo) and Zed (Robbie Magee) from ages five to adulthood as they deal with religious transformations, drug addiction and crime. Filmed in a documentary style using Super-8 footage, *Smack* is actually more fiction than fact.

"It's a little bit of both," says Steve. "Those are real people telling their own stories for the most part. What I've done is recorded a lot people telling stories, five or six of us, transcribed them all onto paper and then made those 150 pages of stories into one linear story where I changed the names, turned the five or six characters into three characters who now are brothers. So it started as a documentary. It's taking original stories and turning them into a fictional context and making them into one story."

Yet elements of the Steve's background and his personal knowledge of the Toronto's 1970s-80s drug culture are in plain view.

"I don't really delve into that as much as I've done with my other work," he insists. "That last character is a surviving junkie and he's telling his own stories. The drug culture is very important here because it's something I knew, and I thought the dramatic appeal would add something compelling to the story. In those days, in the 1970s, the drug culture was much more liberal than it is today. I tried to put that into the perspective. The near-death-defying experience is not exclusive to drug users, and a large part of the story addresses the recklessness of youth, of male youth and some of the underlying factors that might help push somebody in that direction."

After attending Sheridan College, Sanguedolce (which means sweetblood) has dedicated himself to making films using a diary methodology about the darkest and most intimate moments of the person's self. *Full Moon Darkness* (1983) is a portrayal of ex-psychiatric patients; *Woodbridge* (1985) attempted to deconstruct Italian mores; *Rhythms of the Heart* (1990) explored his own issues about romance; *Mexico* (1992) unraveled the world traveler; *Sweetblood* (1993) revisited his family photos; and *Away* (1996) focused on his search for his long-lost twin.

If you've never seen a Sanguedolce film, don't expect a conventional moviegoing experience. Avant-garde and experimental, his movies are a challenge even for seasoned film lovers. And *Smack*, although more accessible than his previous films because of its narrative, is a compendium of hand-processed and hand-toned colourized images.

"My sense of incorporating images is much more metaphorical and poetic," he explains. "When you deal with memory, and most of the film is told in past tense, it becomes coloured in a figurative sense. It's all very specific but unusual. Memory has become something truly unique, it's almost separate from the actual event. I'm more interested in trying to tell stories visually where the images don't necessarily become slaves to the sound. I think that when somebody is speaking about almost dying or being let down, that we're talking about trust and fear and connection, and some of those images deal with a more metaphoric level going either inside or beyond the words. The colouring makes it real specific to a person's recollection, it's more dreamlike and goes beyond what images normally do in dramatic films."

But Sanguedolce's artistry doesn't limit itself to the screen. For years he's been the leader of Sweetblood and the Hounds, a psycho-horror rock band, which plays around Toronto quite often.

"Not anymore," he admits. " I just decided to not play the club circuit anymore. It's too hard and greasy and there's not a lot of rewards. What the bars want is cover music, and original music doesn't fit in there. I feel like I want to try something else. It's the opposite of what cinema is. Cinema is more cerebral. I think I'll leave music behind for now."

Just don't stop making those movies.

Published in Tandem Magazine, *March, 2000.*

FILMOGRAPHY

Born in 1960 in Toronto, Ontario.

- *Smack* (2000)
- *Away* (1996)
- *Sweetblood* (1993)
- *Mexico* (1992)
- *Rhythms of the Heart* (1990)
- *Woodbridge* (1985)
- *Full Moon Darkness* (1983)

STEFAN SCAINI

Under the Piano

He's all over the place, and yet so few of us know about him. Nominated at the Gemini Awards for Best Director, Stefan Scaini has been a mainstay in the Canadian film and television scene for nearly twenty years winning awards world-wide with his short films, and leaving his unique cinematic signature on the many television series he directs.

Although he didn't walk away with the award for *Under the Piano*, fellow Italian-Canadian Jerry Ciccoritti did, his television drama did win three Geminis in other categories. But Scaini seems unfazed by the loss. His dream project is far different from the television stuff he's been making lately.

"I hope to do more indigenous films in my home-town, hopefully about my community," says Scaini, on-line from Los Angeles. "I've been approached by several organizations such as Telefilm, CBC and Republic Pictures to come up with a truly 'Italian' story. That's my ultimate goal. To tell that story that will make our parents, and consequently all of us, laugh and cry. I want to put together a feature film that explores the very unique experiences of our Italian-Canadian culture. It's very different from the Italian-American one as our southern cousins were encouraged to rinse the 'Italian' away quickly and assimilate. Most of my U.S. cousins don't speak Italian and in some cases, changed their names to something more 'American.' Fortunately for us in Canada, we, for the most part, hung on to it. I, for example, speak fluent Friulano and Italian (with a bit of Calabrese thrown in for good measure). My parents and all my relatives made sure we kept the language alive and in doing so, our culture."

And kudos to them for doing so. Having had instilled him since a young boy the pride of immigrant values, Scaini displayed a drive and determination uncommon in most people. At the age of eight, he picked up his dad's Super-8 camera and made a movie for a class project that was received with such success that the young Toronto boy knew he had found his calling.

"I thought 'my goodness, what a way to be able to communicate with people, what a way to engage people and tell a story and reach people,' " remembers Scaini. After enrolling at Ryerson following high school, Scaini quickly discovered that he couldn't get the training he needed to make the movies he wanted to make.

"I was there for one year and there were eight classes of photography and one of film, and I went crazy," says Scaini of Ryerson. "I had to go down to study in California and I couldn't study full-time because I was working as a mechanic as well as working construction with my father. He thought I was nuts, and he thought so up until the day he died. I would study for a stretch of 2-3 weeks, and really learned what it meant to tell a story on film, which is working with the actors and working with a script."

Scaini made his first short film, *The Silent Bell*, when

he was nineteen. The story of a little boy who sees a sick derelict on the street thinking he's Santa Claus went on to win an Actra Award and the New York Film Festival for Best Short Film. His follow-up shorts, *The Calendar Girl* and *A Family Matter,* both dealing with his Italian-Canadian experiences, also won several awards.

"I maintained that style of filmmaking for quite a while where my main priority is the humanities, the characterizations," explains Scaini. "I'm known mostly for melodrama because anytime I can get underneath a person's skin, understand what's happening, I apply it to myself and how I would feel about it. My style of filmmaking is definitely about human beings and about people, and not about car chases or big effects or wonderful imagery."

"My favourite project," says Scaini, "is *Cement Soul.* A wacky black comedy loosely based on people the writer, Tony DiFranco, and I know," he explains. "We've grown up with rich and wonderful experiences through our immigrant parents. The stories are endless. Every time I sit with my mother or relatives, the tales they tell are so engaging, dramatic and at times hysterical that I can't help as a filmmaker to want to tell them so."

Published in Tandem Magazine, *March 1997.*

FILMOGRAPHY

Born in Toronto, Ontario.

- *Myth Quest* (2001)
- *Happy Christmas, Miss King* (1998)
- *Lyddie* (1996)
- *Under the Piano* (1995)
- *I'll Never Get to Heaven* (1992)

SCOTT THOMPSON

Brain Candy

Scott Thompson has not had the easiest time being a celebrity. Hardly one to keep his opinions to himself, he's been snubbed by the gay media for his off-the-cuff remarks about *Philadelphia* a few years ago, the movie starring the very married and heterosexual Tom Hanks and Denzel Washington.

At the time Thompson told *Variety* that he believed filmmakers should only hire gay actors to portray gay characters, a comment most would agreed was self-defacing and immature.

"I did go after *Philadelphia*," remembers Thompson on-line from Los Angeles. "I think it has caused me problems. Some of the things that I've said have caused me real problems. I don't regret any of it but it's made it harder for me. I think if I had kept my mouth shut I'd be doing better and I'd be getting more scripts. But I don't care. The sad thing about it is that some of the things that I've said put a lot of gay people's noses out of joint, a lot of gay people who are in power. We should be helping each other but that's not the case. But I prefer to leave that alone, now. I'm tired of it, I've already got my ulcer."

No kidding. Since the break-up of the *Kids in the Hall* several years ago, Thompson has been running around the continent doing comedy shows and landing a coveted regular spot on the critically acclaimed, and highly awarded HBO TV satire *The Larry Sanders Show,* a job he got without even having to audition.

"I basically had to make Gary Shandling a cup of coffee and I got the job. It was that simple," he laughs. "He got a hold of me when I was in Turkey, and I was recovering in the hotel from a bad burn that I got in a Turkish bath. My manager got a hold of me and said that Gary Shandling wanted to meet me, so I flew to Los Angeles and he offered me the job on the spot."

Although he's pleased to be appearing on one of the most respected shows on television, and portraying a gay character nonetheless, Thompson is hoping to do some writing for Shandling some day.

"I don't think it's going to happen that easily," he says. "I really would love to but I think what I'm going to hopefully be able to do is meet with the writers first, and hopefully be able to have more of an input. I would love to write an episode but I don't think that's in the cards. But I'm sure this year my character will get more developed and I'll be able to have more of a say. It's a very good show but I'm not used to being on the periphery, so that's kind of hard for me. It's got a great atmosphere. It doesn't matter where the idea comes from, if it's good he'll use it. I really admire that."

But the cause of Thompson's anxiety and stress stems not from the *Sanders Show* or the hostility by the gay community, but from *The Kids in the Hall* reunion film, *Brain Candy.* After six seasons producing the television hit series, the five members had considerably fallen out of touch with each other (Dave Foley stars in the NBC series *News Radio*; Bruce McCulloch writes plays; Kevin

McDonald just starred in *National Lampoon's Senior Trip* and Mark McKinney is a regular on *Saturday Night Live*).

"It was hard, the writing part was extremely hard because we were writing as a group again and it had been years since we've done that," remembers Thompson. "It was difficult making people's schedules come together. But the actual filming of the movie was wonderful. I wish that that could've gone on forever. When we're acting between 'action' and 'cut,' I'm never happier but a lot of the things around it didn't make me happy and dealing with the studio was not something it was really rough. They tried to intervene with the creative process.

"But there were definitely fault lines in the group that had widened. It's no secret that we became estranged from Dave. But we've been talking and we've been working a lot of that out. We're like an old married couple but we know that what we do is really good so we kind of always ignore the pain that we cause each other."

Pain also reached Thompson in a more personal way. Two weeks before filming began, Thompson's brother committed suicide casting doubts on the comedian's ability to carry on with the film.

"I didn't think I was going to be able to do it," he says. "What happened was, the movie, in many ways for me, became my therapy. I'll never get over what happened. I think about it every day. It's changed me tremendously. We were a year apart. It was so weird because I never wanted the day to end. I didn't want to leave my character. What made things weirder was that a lot of the things in the movie had a lot to do with my brother's life. The movie is about depression, drugs, and there's even a character in the film that's sort of based on my brother. So I look at the movie and it's painful. Kevin was also going through a hard time [divorce] and we really helped each other a lot during that period."

Although all the members admit to missing the *Hall* they all agree that they'd run out steam and it was time to move on. A native of North Bay, Ontario, Thompson was the last member to join the Toronto comedy troupe in 1984.

"They used to see me at Theatresports with my team, The Lovecats," says Thompson. "We were notorious for being notorious, we weren't particularly great but we were very funny. They asked me to do a guest spot with them, and I did. Then they asked me to do another one, and I just never went away. The first time I saw them I knew I was going to be in that group, I had a flash and I just kept hanging around. At the beginning, of course, I did all the thankless roles then I started writing and once they realized that I could write, they asked me to join."

Was the success a surprise?

"I guess," he laughs. "It sounds arrogant but I really did think we would be successful, I just knew it in my heart. The thing is I actually thought we would be bigger, I actually thought that we would break and we never actually broke, and our movie didn't break us. I'm disappointed about that."

The reason being, most believe, is that their material is too strong for the public at this stage. In fact, it was Thompson who introduced the now-signature cross-dressing sketches to the show causing countless headaches for the CBC censors.

"We just scared them, we were real tigers about defending our work," says Thompson. "I think when people go to the wall for what they believe in, others are really impressed. A lot of the areas of comedy that we went into were very new and people weren't doing comedy about that kind of stuff so a lot of the censors didn't really know how to counteract our arguments. They never really had this kind of argument before and I know, for myself, I used a lot of guilt. I definitely played very dirty in terms of gay stuff they didn't want in. I employed their liberal guilt. I would accuse them of having double standards and the worst thing you can do is accuse a liberal of prejudice. I went pretty low, I have to admit. I would do anything to get what I want on TV."

Which didn't go always so well with the other Kids.

"It was a slow process," admits Thompson. "At the beginning I had to really prove myself over and over again, but a couple of years into the group people were really accepting of it. As straight guys there was a kind of a thrill for them to put on dresses and kiss each other and fuck people's butts. Much like a rock band would've. I know, for myself, I never saw anything wrong with it and I was never embarrassed and never hesitated to get into drag because for me it was a very natural way to say things that I couldn't say normally or say as a man. I think for some of the others it wasn't as natural but eventually they really got into it especially when they saw how pretty they were."

As for what the future has in store for Thompson, aside from *The Larry Sanders Show,* he's just finished filming *Hijacking Hollywood* with ET child star, now man, Henry Thomas.

"I play a production coordinator on a big Hollywood movie who harasses a young production assistant," explains Thompson. "This PA and his pal steal a roll of film that's unbelievably expensive because it's a day where they had big special effects so it's worth millions of dollars. They steal it and they hold it for ransom and I try to get it back. I play a real prick."

Borrowing from experience?

"Being a prick?" he laughs. "No. But as far as being harassed, sure' we had some pretty scary people in our past."

Another big project on Thompson's plate is the highly hyped and talked-about Scottland (www.scottland.com), one of the coolest websites on the net right now. Closer to an episodic television show than a traditional information site, Scottland features many of Thompson's characters as they develop their own universe.

"I wanted something where I felt I didn't know what I was doing," says Thompson. "I thought it would be fun to do something that was so unregulated and lawless and my brother, Craig, was quitting his job as an engineer at Hydro, and he wanted to start a company for websites and he asked me if I wanted to be the first one. So we decided to do it together. I had a lot of free time on my hands when we first did it so I thought it was cool. It's a new kind of non-linear entertainment."

What Scott didn't anticipate, however, was the considerable expense at running a website.

"Oh, yeah," he sighs. "I'm not making any money. It's cost me my savings but I think it's going to be worth it. We're trying to get sponsors and we've had some nibbles from some pretty big people that are interested in developing it. I like to develop it and do some sort of a pilot, sort of television, sort of a magazine, sort of a book, sort of an album."

Sort of a Scott Thompson.

Published in Menz Magazine, *August 1996.*

FILMOGRAPHY

Born June 12, 1959, in North Bay, Ontario.

- *Run, Ronnie, Run* (2002)
- *Tart* (2001)
- *Mickey Blue Eyes* (1999)
- *Hijacking Hollywood* (1997)
- *Hayseed* (1997)
- *Kids in the Hall: Brain Candy* (1996)
- *Out: Stories of Lesbian and Gay Youth in Canada* (1994)
- *Super 8-1/2* (1993)
- *Millennium* (1989)
- *Head Office* (1986)

CLEMENT VIRGO

Love Come Down

When I first saw Clement Virgo's 1992 Canadian Film Festival short *Save My Lost Nigga' Soul* a reworking of the Cain and Abel tale where Cain is a drug addict and Abel is his disapproving brother, I was taken by the young filmmaker's profound sense of community. Although Virgo would expand on this theme of cultural and urban displacement three years later with his terrific first feature *Rude*, extending *Soul*'s story was always in the back of his mind.

"When I wrote *Save My Lost Nigga' Soul*, it was supposed to be a feature film," admits Virgo whose *Love Come Down* makes its world premiere at the Toronto International Film Festival. "I think the script evolved. When I first made it, all the characters were metaphors in some way. One brother represented Cain, the other brother was Abel, and I wanted to bring them more into the real world. I also wanted to make it more personal. Over the last two years, as a filmmaker, and as an artist, I was trying to figure out what I was feeling and what I was going through. I was really trying to come to terms with what I was really feeling about myself and I how I feel about the world."

And what did he conclude?

"One of the characters in the film says it's about love. It's a kind of way of reacting to the world," he explains.

"Either you accept the unknown or you fight against it. It's a way of being in the world. For me it's really about having compassion for yourself and compassion for others."

Love Come Down, Virgo's third feature film (his second, *The Planet of Junior Brown*, was a made-for-TV movie) is the tale of two brothers in their early twenties, one black, one white. Neville (Larenz Tate) is a comedian struggling with his comedy, and his brother, Matthew (Martin Cummins), is a boxer content with who he is. Along the way, Neville becomes enchanted with Niko (Deborah Cox), a young singer who helps him on his journey of self-discovery. With the support of their long-time friend, Julian (Rainbow Sun Francks), and Sister Sarah (Sarah Polley), a nun with a past, Neville and Matthew come to terms with each other."

"The movie is really a meditation about love, love in all of its forms," says Virgo. "Romantic love, self love, family love. It's about someone who's truly learning how to love."

Despite the fact that it took Virgo over five years to get *Love Come Down* off the ground ("raising $3 million in this country isn't easy"), his confidence as a filmmaker was getting stronger, something that reflects greatly in this film.

"*Rude* is about me; *Rude* is very stylish and very flashy in-your-face," he explains. "Part of the experience of *Rude* is watching the movie, the sighs and sounds and whistles and bells of the film. *Love Come Down* is much more subtle than that. I think it's more mature, and it's about the film, it's not about me. It's about the story and about the characters. And I think the film engages the audience on a much more emotional level and on an intellectual level."

As well as cultural.

"It might be presumption, but I think the film is a 21st century Toronto film," agrees Virgo. "I think the city represents a kind of cultural mosaic of what the future is supposed to look like, at least how I thought about it as a child. A mix of people and cultures, rich in gaps."

Published in Word Magazine, *September 2000.*

FILMOGRAPHY

Born in Jamaica.

- *Love Come Down* (2000)
- *One Heart Broken Into Song* (1999)
- *The Planet of Junior Brown* (1997)
- *Rude* (1995)
- *Save My Lost Nigga Soul* (1993)
- *Split Second Pullout Technique* (1992)
- *A Small Dick Fleshy Ass Thang* (1991)

STEPHEN WILLIAMS

Soul Survivor

It's a crucial moment in the filming of *Soul Survivor* and director Stephen Williams finds himself unexpectedly perturbed. The movie's main character, Tyrone, has just discovered his best friend's death and breaks down into anguished tears. The actor, and the director's brother, Peter Williams seems genuinely distraught prompting Stephen to stop the take and whisper to him, "I'm sorry, I'm so sorry to put you through that."

Although he's insisted since pre-production that working with his brother would be no different from working with any other actor, Williams admits that there were moments where objectivity just flies in the face of the wind.

"It was really hard, it was really painful to watch," says Stephen during the lunch break. "Again, I would have felt that for any actor, but more so because he's my brother. I felt badly that I put him through that but the scene required that kind of emotional response and we had to do it. That took me by surprise. We shot a love scene, for instance, and it didn't feel any different than shooting a love scene with any actor, but for some reason this one here of him crying was painful to witness."

We're sure Peter's forgiven him, especially considering that *Soul Survivor* went on to open the prestigious Critics Week at the Cannes Film Festival this year (one of

seven films selected from an approximate 800 considered!). As for Stephen, seeing his first feature film pre-
miered at the world's largest film festival was, in his
words, "a humbling experience."

But even more satisfying, Williams says, was the level
of journalistic interrogation by French journalists who
displayed an understanding of his film many Canadian
critics failed to exhibit.

"They were very interested in so many other dimen-
sions of the film," explains Stephen over lunch in Toronto
a week after returning from Cannes. "We tried to make a
multi-layered film and it's often disheartening to run
across journalists whose only preoccupation was how
hard it was working with my brother. The French were,
for the most part, very interested in all the elements that
came together to make *Soul Survivor* what it is. They were
intrigued by the way the film challenged their perceived
notions of what constituted demographic reality in Canada. They had no idea that there were so many Black
people here and that there was as vibrant a Jamaican
immigrant culture here. That naturally opened into all
kinds of questions I hope the film raises around notions
of immigration."

That and much more. Like his stylish Canadian Film
Centre short, *A Variation on the Key 2 Life*, which posed
the question "What price art?", Williams tip-toes around
the main notion in *Soul Survivor*, that in life we all have
a price to pay, to delve deep into the intricate patterns
that shape our society: issues of identity, and notions of
home, struggle and racism.

Set in the heart of Toronto's Jamaican community,

Soul Survivor revolves around Tyrone Taylor, an ambitious hairdresser who takes a job collecting debts for local money lender Winston (George Harris). Tyrone has just rekindled a relationship with social worker Annie (Judith Scott) but worries about the foolish and dangerous antics of his best friend, Reuben (David Smith).

"The germ of Tyrone and his journey came out of my own experiences when I first came to Toronto and was faced with similar kinds of things," explains Williams who moved to T.O. as a teenager from Jamaica via England. "How do I make my way in this culture without losing so much of what I valued about my culture that I brought with me? How do I reconcile those two things? My cultural inheritance from Jamaica involves a very healthy spiritual and moral dimension. When I came to North America those kind of things, because they're intangible and are hard to package and commodify and sell, have very little currency here. The dilemma that I faced was how do I make sense of these two different ways of being in the world? So the germ of the character came from there, then imagination came into play."

As the movie unfolds so does Tyrone's growing awareness of his place in the world. It's this attempt to deal with certain archetypal notions of self-awareness that make *Soul Survivor* a mesmerizing and enriching experience to watch. Just as the human drama is heightened by luxurious colours, blood reds, raven blacks, the viewer's attention to detail is also elevated to absorb the subtle and intelligent characterizations which authenticates further the events presented.

"What I didn't want to do is present a film where the metaphysical penny has dropped and now the character knows exactly what he's going to do," explains Williams. "It doesn't strike me, certainly in terms of my own life, that that's actually what happens. I think we change through a series of increments rather than all at one fell swoop. Throughout the course of the movie this character attempts to reconcile some really irreconcilable things like loyalty on the one hand to cousin Reuben, and expedience on the other, getting ahead materially. In the end we are left with the character who has come out understanding that that kind of juggling act is dangerous and untenable in every way. For me the film was more than a social document. For me there was a metaphysical component to it, a presentation of ideas in collision with each other. When we leave Tyrone at the end of the movie these ideas have in fact collided in his world in a very real way."

Funded by the Ontario Film Development Corporation and Telefilm Canada, *Soul Survivor* was not an easy project to get off the ground. Unlike his Film Centre pal and fellow Cannes-ter Clement Virgo, whose film, *Rude*, was financed by the Centre's Feature Film Project, Williams had to scramble from the bottom up to find dough for his pic. Thanks to the support of influential producer Paul Brown (*I Love A Man in Uniform*), *Soul Survivor* has become the second film to be produced under the Miracle Pictures banner.

While Williams is completely satisfied with the attention his film has received at film festivals worldwide, he confesses that the project's outcome is not as important as the personal catharsis that occurred during the actual production.

"In many ways the making of the movie mirrored the content of the film," he explains. "What am I prepared to trade as a human being in order to get to make a film? In many ways it was in the back of my mind the quasi-Faustian pact that Tyrone makes with Winston, his benefactor. In many ways, for me, that mirrored the kind of process I was going through in terms of developing this project. It was interesting to me that overlap. It was the level of ideas as opposed to social reality. That whole journey absolutely I feel an emotional and spiritual kinship with, attempting to examine your life as you go through it to figure out how you can retain the vestiges of your own spiritual orientation at the same time as being in the world."

For those of us who have followed Williams' career closely for the past several years, this talk of spiritual and emotional awareness is hardly new. An artist in its purest form, Williams has displayed an unconditional love and commitment to his craft like few people this writer has ever encountered. Williams has often expressed the need to display his unique perspective of reality through his own visualization without having to compromise technical or artistic freedom.

"In some way I need to find a visual kind of way of retrenching the way in which I experience the world which, I think, is idiosyncratic," he once explained in his trademark eloquence. "For me reality is a very negotiable item. A collision of subjectivities is what makes reality. I don't really think much about things being objectively real. I'm trying to grapple with a way of giving expression to that."

Asked whether *Soul Survivor* is an extension of that philosophy and whether the experience of watching it has overwhelmed him yet, Williams shrugs.

"I can't watch the movie. I've seen it so many times it's unintelligible to me," he says. "While I'm proud of the movie I don't dwell on the film. My sense of who I am is not inextricably bound up with what the movie is and how well it does and what the movie's trajectory is. Those are two separate entities that overlap each other but that are quite distinct in my own psyche. The movie was really about the experience of leveraging that collective energy that we all brought to the making of the movie. One hopes that at the end of it it's a semi coherent document that touches other people other than ourselves. That's the real experience, truly. Everything else is gravy. Cannes is gravy, Sundance is gravy, Toronto is gravy."

Would he go through it again?

"Yes," he smiles. "Nothing I do satisfies me. Somehow that makes me want to keep doing it, keep making films. To watch the movie, every scene reminds me of how short I have fallen and how uninspired and uninspiring I am. I get bogged down by my inabilities, and then I think that I can do better and I should do better. As you can see, I'm a very cheery guy."

Published in Take 1 Magazine, *June 1995.*

Born in Jamaica.

- *A Killing Spree* (2002)
- *Harry's Case* (1999)
- *Milgaard* (1999)
- Shadow Zone: My Teacher Ate My Homework (1997)
- *Soul Survivor* (1995)
- *A Variation on the Key 2 Life* (1993)

MICHAEL ZELNIKER

Stuart Bliss

Stuart Bliss is one of those indie gems that makes a movie lover grateful there are filmmakers out there still willing to take chances. This story about a man who becomes overwhelmed with feelings of paranoia and persecution to the point of destroying his life, is the brainchild of first-time director Neil Grieve and Montreal-born actor Michael Zeniker.

How did this disquieting tale of paranoia come to mind?

The original script was actually written by director Neil Grieve. It was more a story simply about a man going crazy and that interested me less than exploring the fine line between, The subtitle to the film is "Just because he's paranoid doesn't mean they're not after him." We don't see those as mutually exclusive ideas. One can be paranoid and they can be after us at the same time and that's where we think there can be some humour. Albeit a black comedy, but exploring what sometimes are seemingly contrary notions and seeing how, in fact, they can operate simultaneously. That's an idea that's interesting and I think compels humour.

When you decided to put this project together, how difficult was it getting financing?

I think one of the problems that the larger, more orthodox filmmaking enterprises have with a movie like

Stuart Bliss is that it's original. Sometimes machineries that are very well entrenched don't necessarily know how to fathom and then market and conceive of a truly original idea. Rather than go through the huge frustration about having someone invite Neil to make a film, he decided to try and make this movie himself. He wrote script, he knew my work as an actor and approached me thinking that I was right for the role. That's how I got involved rewriting it Neil, I liked the concept but felt that within the seed of the idea, there was a much more interesting way to run with the story and that's how we got involved rewriting it together.

But you sent the script to some major studios?

At that stage then we actually sent it out to some people who were willing to read it. And that was quite exciting. As you know I've worked primarily as an actor and this was my first foray into writing, so to have large production companies like Paramount and DreamWorks interested even in reading the script, was very exciting to me. It was almost like in the days of my first audition. But what we got back was: "A truly original idea, very exciting. We'd be interesting in doing something with it but with a first-time director and an actor attached in the central role who doesn't have a big commercial name, you'd have to give that away." Of course that wasn't what we were interested in doing. The whole premise about putting this together for Neil and I was to offer him an opportunity to direct it and for me to play this wonderful role.

Los Angeles is a surreal city. Could Stuart Bliss *have been set anywhere else?*

I think it can be set in other cities. I think there's a universal application to it, but I do think the specifics of what you refer to are unique to Los Angeles, to Los Angeles living, gave it a really great resonance. It allowed it to work really well with this story. But I always believe that it's not just a few wackos living in Montana who believe that with the coming millennium that the world is coming to an end. There's a lot of panic out there. I know that it's kind of underneath the radar, but there's a lot of people concerned. It's manifested in some ways with this Y2K concern, you know? But there are a lot of people stocking up on foodstuffs, and as we get closer to the millennium there are a lot of people concerned about.

You make fun of this fear in Stuart Bliss *though.*

Well, it became an opportunity to make some fun in a loving way. As we make fun of Stuart's growing paranoia through the film, there's very much the concept involved, at least in my mind, that yes indeed, Stuart does come to believe that the world is coming to an end, but with the stuff that's happening to him who can blame him? Wouldn't any of us start to believe that there's something awry going on here? That's a very important part. Neil and I knew in making this film that if we didn't allow the viewer to experience the film through Stuart's experiences, the film could never be successful. So for me playing Stuart as much as anything, what I was thinking was I never believed that he was paranoid, I never believed that I was paranoid playing Stuart.

What were you aware of?

That he came to take everything very, very personally, like a level of narcissism that became almost pathological.

But that all sounds very serious. For me the movie really is quite funny, and from the festivals we've been to audiences tend to agree. But it's always very tricky making a black comedy because black comedy means you're dealing with a serious subject and trying to find the humour in it. I think it's easy to imagine that Neil and I at times both felt paranoid because making a black comedy about paranoia can make you feel a little nervous.

For most viewers, however, it doesn't matter if what's happening to Stuart is real or not.

On that subject I'm more interested in art in general, if it leaves something to the viewer, that there's some work to be done by the viewer. In other words we didn't want to leave the audience with conclusions, we wanted to leave them with a lot of relevant questions. For the audience then to come out of the screening questioning "Was Stuart just crazy? Was stuff really happening?" debating those questions are interesting to me.

Following the success of Stuart Bliss, *are you guys being sought after by the biggies now?*

We were fortunate enough to be invited to a lot of festivals, we won a couple of best film awards and it gave us the opportunity to play the film in front of a wide variety of audiences. We've also gotten awesome reviews. But what happens in this business is that people are loath to say yes until somebody else in the business says yes. So we're waiting.

Published in Tandem Magazine, *July 1999.*

FILMOGRAPHY

Born in Montreal, Quebec.

- *Rats* (2001)
- After Image (2000)
- *Nostradamus* (2000)
- *Stuart Bliss* (1998)
- *Toxic Remedy* (1997)
- *Within the Rock* (1996)
- *Night Canvas* (1995)
- *Queens Logic* (1991)
- *Naked Lunch* (1991)
- *Bird* (1988)
- *Touch and Go* (1986)
- *Eleni* (1985)
- *Ticket to Heaven* (1981)
- *Heartaches* (1981)
- *Pick-up Summer* (1980)
- *Hog Wild* (1980)

MEMBRE DE SCABRINI MEDIA

Québec, Canada
2002